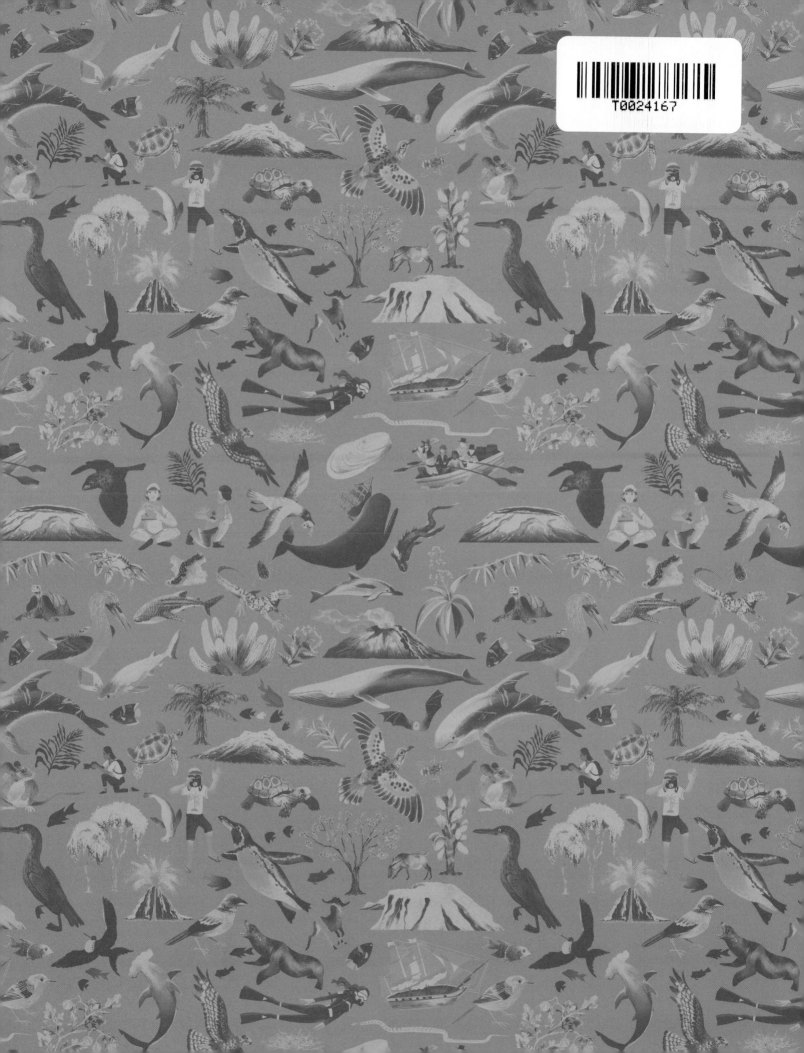

EARTH'S
EXTRAORDINARY
PLACES

GALÁPAGOS

Foreword by
STEVE BACKSHALL

Written by
TOM JACKSON

Illustrated by
CHERVELLE FRYER

Contents

Marine life

Plants

People and preservation

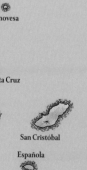

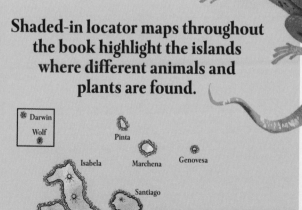

Shaded-in locator maps throughout the book highlight the islands where different animals and plants are found.

Darwin
Wolf
Pinta
Isabela
Marchena
Genovesa
Santiago
Santa Cruz
Fernandina
Floreana
San Cristóbal
Española

Foreword

Steve Backshall, MBE

A swarm of black salt-encrusted dinosaurs lie basking on a volcanic rock. White spume crashes over them, from waves that have traveled thousands of miles across the entire Pacific. Smaller lava lizards sit on their heads, reveling in their living deck chairs. As the equatorial sun rises in the sky, the marine iguanas lift themselves imperceptibly from their slumber, and take a leisurely waddle down the rock. They plop over the side, and into the crashing swell. Once underwater, they transform, swimming in eel-like dark shapes down to the rocks below. Using their pointed curved talons, they cling to tiny imperfections in the rock, and use their short, blunt snouts to gnaw green slime from the boulders. Engrossed in their task, they allow me to get within reach, even briefly glancing up to look at their own reflections in my mask.

There is nowhere else on Earth you can have this experience. There is no other place where lizards high dive into the sea to feed. But here in the Galápagos, to be unique is not unique. In fact, it is the norm. Marine iguanas are just one of more than two thousand species found nowhere else.

Many of the finest wildlife experiences of my career have been here in these wind- and wave-smashed seamounts, on the outer rim of the Ring of Fire. Underwater I've danced with sea lions, spinning and pirouetting around me in a weightless ballet that is (quite literally) breathless. I've been lucky enough to lie on the seabed, nose to nose with a red-lipped batfish. The weirdest fish in our oceans? Possibly.

There is enough written in these pages about Darwin, his love affair with these islands, and how that led to the development of the biggest and most important idea in biology. Too often commentators act as if the importance of Galápagos is all historical, rather than NOW. However, new species are still being discovered; with one single recent expedition coming back with thirty new species, including new corals and other invertebrates. The process of evolution still continues here, with evolutionary biologists tracking the changes in real time of the finches Darwin so treasured. Around the time I was born, black smokers, or hydrothermal vents, were discovered off the coast of Galápagos.

A group of marine iguanas using the sky-pointing posture to cool down on the shore of Fernandina Island.

Not just a new species, but an entire new ecosystem that was new to science. Less than a decade later, and scientists were starting to realize how important this new environment is. In fact, the dominant hypothesis now is that life on our planet first began at these seemingly inhospitable islands.

But while I am lucky enough to have had some of my greatest wildlife experiences here, I have also had my most melancholy experiences with nature here. We had been one of the last film crews to record Lonesome George, the last ever Pinta Island tortoise. When I had met George, he was at least a hundred years old, grizzled, gnarled, and wrinkled. He had been alone for my entire lifetime. His kind had been hunted by fishermen who took all they wanted with no thoughts of what might be sustainable. Now he is gone, and with him his entire species. I have also been out diving at the volcanic seamounts; the finest sites for sights on marine aggregation in the world. In theory these seamounts are no-take zones, yet we witnessed fishing vessels just waiting for us to leave, so they could come in and plunder the treasures of this vast national park. An industrial foreign fishing fleet of hundreds of boats has hovered around the outskirts of (and often well within) the boundaries of the park, catching tens of thousands of tons of marine life, and putting impossible pressure on the marine life of this global treasure.

The Galápagos faces vast challenges. But to stroll along a beach and see a sea lion mother giving birth to a pup, fighting to drive off the frigate birds as they swoop to steal the afterbirth; to swim in a silvery bait ball of tiny fish, with penguins sweeping and swooping like torpedoes; to watch tropicbirds in the crashing spray of the surf, with their white streamers fluttering like kite tails behind them. . .there is nowhere else on Earth you can see these things.

These islands are as precious now as they have ever been.

Steve Backshall, MBE

BAFTA-winning wildlife presenter,
naturalist, and explorer

Alcedo giant tortoises are the only species of giant tortoise to make Volcano Alcedo their home.

Introduction

Welcome to the Galápagos! These islands of sand and lava, nestled in the Pacific Ocean, are a treasure trove of amazing stories.

They tell of mighty volcanic blasts and mysterious undersea vents. Other tales talk of brave explorers who strayed far out to sea to find these remote lands, which then became a haven for pirates and even a prison. Today, visitors come to marvel at the incredible wildlife, including the unforgettable giant tortoises. Early Spanish sailors noted the saddle-shaped shells of some of these tortoises. This is how the islands got their name—"Galápagos" comes from an old Spanish word for a horse saddle. The most famous visitor to the islands was Charles Darwin, whose observations led him to make a scientific discovery that changed the world.

Galápagos superstars

Cut off from the rest of the world, the Galápagos Islands have a very special community of wildlife. Here are some of the most spectacular species.

Blue-footed booby

Famed for its big blue feet, this seabird can be seen dancing on the shore.

Brand-new lands

A special feature of the Galápagos Islands is their origin—they appeared out of nowhere. Over millions of years, undersea volcanoes threw out fire and lava onto the seabed. This created layers of rock that grew and grew until they broke above the surface, forming islands in the ocean. The new land was completely bare, but ready for life to get a foothold.

Natural wonders

Little by little, life arrived on the empty islands from across the ocean. Isolated from the rest of the world for many millions of years, the islands didn't have the same big trees, large hunting mammals, and other species common on the South American mainland. As a result, the Galápagos developed a unique set of wildlife that did things differently.

Marine iguana

This is a lizard with a big difference—it feeds on algae on rocks in the sea that are close to the shore. No other lizard lives this way!

Giant tortoises

Immense and slow-moving, these big beasts have made a life for themselves all over the islands.

Lava cactus

Don't touch! This spiky plant grows slowly out of the dry rock fields made from cooled lava.

Túpac Yupanqui

Legend has it that this Inca emperor led the first expedition to the Galápagos Islands in 1480.

Scalloped hammerhead

Many species of sharks, including this hammerhead, come in their thousands to the waters around the islands each year.

Flightless cormorant

A bird built for swimming rather than flying, this big, dark diver is unique to the Galápagos Islands.

Charles Darwin

This English naturalist's visit to the Galápagos Islands in 1835 made them world famous.

Daisy trees

The biggest trees on the islands are more closely related to daisies than oak or pine trees.

Cradle of science

Charles Darwin explained how the animals and plants that arrived on the Galápagos were able to change to suit the new conditions they found themselves in. Darwin's theory of evolution transformed science and changed the way people saw themselves and nature. Today, the islands are still an important center for scientific research.

Protection needed

People have been living on the Galápagos islands for around two hundred years. In that time, much of the amazing nature living there has been harmed. Settlers have cleared the natural habitats to create farms and have introduced many animals and plants that are now taking over or killing the island's original wildlife. The islands need our help to prevent further damage.

Darwin

These two islands are the remains of long-extinct volcanoes—they last erupted over 400,000 years ago. Darwin and Wolf Islands are more than 190 miles (306 km) away from the central islands. Wolf Island is 78 miles (125 km) from Redonda.

Wolf

Redonda

Pinta

Marchena

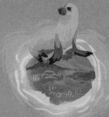

Santiago

Sometimes known as San Salvador, this island was once a single large volcano. Much of the island is covered in a lava flow that erupted a few centuries ago. In 1835, explorers from the *Beagle* discovered marmalade jars, dating from 1684, embedded in the lava. They were left behind by pirates.

Bartolomé

Baltra

Rábida

Fernandina

The youngest island in the group, Fernandina has a highly active volcano with the tallest peak in the Galápagos. The island is named after Ferdinand II of Aragon, the Spanish king who sponsored Columbus's first voyage to the Americas. Fernandina is home to many marine iguanas, Galápagos penguins, and flightless cormorants.

Pinzón

Santa Cruz

This island at the center of the archipelago is where most of the people in the Galápagos live, especially in the town of Puerto Ayora. Just north of Santa Cruz lies the small island of Baltra, home to the islands' main airport. Santa Cruz's central volcano is at least a million years old—perhaps older—and it hasn't erupted significantly for more than 700,000 years.

Tortuga

Isabela

The largest island in the archipelago, Isabela makes up more than half of all the land in the Galápagos. It is four times larger than the next biggest island, Santa Cruz. The island is named after Queen Isabella I of Castile, who ruled Spain with her husband Ferdinand II. There are six volcanoes on the island (five of which are currently active), and it's home to more wild giant tortoises than anywhere else in the world.

Floreana

Floreana was the first island inhabited by humans in the Galápagos. Today, most of the people living here are farmers. A lot of conservation work also takes place on the island.

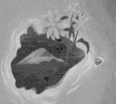

Galápagos

Genovesa
Nicknamed "Bird Island" since it's home to masses of seabirds, this island is much younger than its nearest neighbors. There were major eruptions here around six thousand years ago, creating a saltwater crater lake at the island's center.

The Galápagos is an archipelago, or chain of islands, that stretches across 17,000 sq miles (45,000 sq km) of ocean. Only around 18 percent of this is made of land, which is around the same amount of land as Greece.

There is a total of 128 islands in the Galápagos Archipelago. However, around 110 of them are just tiny islets—very small islands with no vegetation—poking out of the ocean. The main islands make up most of the land, and new land is regularly created with each eruption of the islands' many volcanoes.

San Cristóbal
Named after Saint Christopher, the patron saint of sailors, this island is formed from the remains of three or four long-extinct volcanoes. At the time of Darwin's visit, San Cristóbal was being used as a penal colony—a remote place to send prisoners.

Santa Fé
This small island was a volcano. Its crater is now under the sea. It was formed by an uplift of rock from the seabed, making it flat, unlike the other islands!

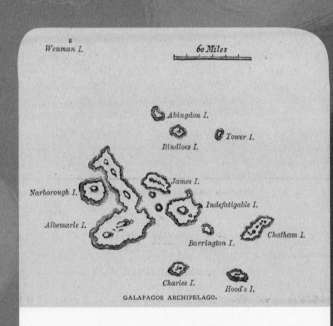

Darwin's map
Charles Darwin sketched a map of the Galápagos during his exploration of the islands in 1835. He later included the sketch (above) in his book on the voyage. Darwin used English names for the islands. *Santa Cruz* was then known as *Indefatigable* and *San Cristóbal* was named *Chatham*, after the English seaport, which was then a major naval base. At that time, the small island that now bears Darwin's name was called *Culpepper* (not shown above). Darwin and other members of the *Beagle*'s crew visited most of the islands, and one of their jobs was to update the naval charts of the region.

Española
At around four million years old, Española is probably the oldest island in the archipelago. It's known for its colony of albatross.

The hotspot in action

The Galápagos Islands are still being created. They are made by a volcanic system called a hotspot—a plume of hot magma (molten rock) deep beneath the islands. The hotspot feeds the islands' many volcanoes, adding new land with every eruption of lava.

Over millions of years, the seabed and the islands on top of it have been on the move, very slowly drifting sideways. The hotspot, however, has stayed where it is. So, as older islands move out of the way, lava from new volcanoes above the hotspot builds more islands in their place. This gradually creates the chain of islands we call the Galápagos.

Lava is the name for magma once it's left the volcano. It cools and hardens to form new land.

In time, plants and wildlife take over a volcanic island.

Plate movement

The seabed and the Galápagos Islands are part of a section of Earth's crust, called a tectonic plate. This plate has been moving southeast toward South America at around 2 in (5 cm) a year— that's roughly the same rate your fingernails grow. The plate's movement shifts older islands away from the hotspot, deep below the crust in the mantle.

Island

Hot liquid rock is called magma when it's still underground.

Plate movement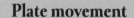

Hotspot

Crust

Hotspot

Lava from the Galápagos hotspot has been building the islands for the last 4.5 million years. As well as the islands we see today, the hotspot created former volcanoes, now drowned seamounts. The seabed around the islands is also covered in a volcanic platform that's 2 miles (3 km) deep. This was created by lava gradually spreading across the seabed from around 20 million years ago.

Mantle

Nazca Plate

The Galápagos Islands sit on a section of crust called the Nazca Plate. There's a mid-ocean ridge running between this plate and the plates on its northern and western edges. Lava pushes up along this and forms new seabed. This process pushes the Nazca Plate toward South America. At its eastern edge, the Nazca Plate plunges under the continent of South America, where its rocks melt into the mantle.

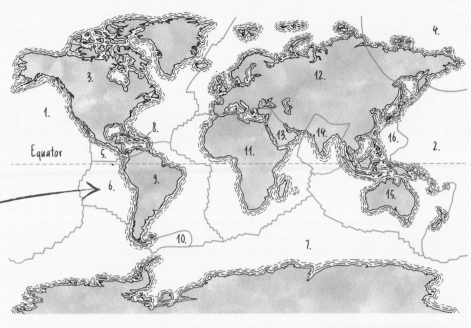

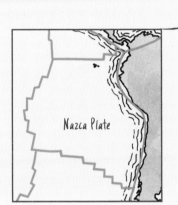

1. & 2. Pacific Plate 3. & 4. North American Plate 5. Cocos Plate 6. Nazca Plate 7. Antarctic Plate
8. Caribbean Plate 9. South American Plate 10. Scotia Plate 11. African Plate 12. Eurasian Plate
13. Arabian Plate 14. Indian Plate 15. Indo-Australian Plate 16. Philippine Plate

Island chain

As an island moves farther from the hotspot, its volcanoes become less active and are eventually cut off from the supply of magma. Without fresh eruptions of lava, the islands cannot grow larger. Instead, they start to shrink as their tall volcanic mountains are worn away by the rain, wind, and waves.

Earth's crust is not a single shell of rock. It is broken into many sections, called plates.

Older islands will eventually disappear under the sea.

The oldest Galápagos Island is at the eastern end of the chain.

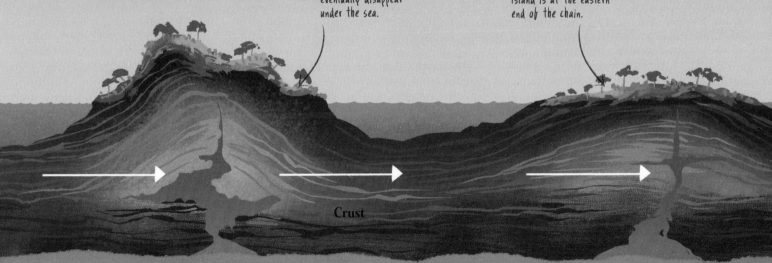

Crust

Mantle

The hotspot's position is below the Earth's crust in a deeper layer of our planet, called the mantle. The mantle is made of hot, rocky materials, but it's not all rock solid like the crust. The Galápagos hotspot is a plume of liquid magma that has bubbled up from a hotter part of the mantle, even deeper down.

The volcanoes
of the Galápagos

Lava erupts on Isabela Island.

The Galápagos Islands are volcanic in origin. Evidence of past and present eruptions is clear to see from the islands' many volcanoes. There are twenty-one separate volcanoes above sea level. Some are tall peaks that dominate their islands; others are now extinct with just the peaks of their prehistoric craters peeking above the ocean as small islands.

Volcanoes may be active, dormant, or extinct. Six of the Galápagos Islands' volcanoes are active, with regular eruptions in recent years. Several others are dormant—they haven't erupted for a long time, but may do so in the future. The rest are extinct and will never erupt again since they have moved too far from the Galápagos hotspot and its supply of magma. The most active peaks tend to be the youngest and largest volcanoes. The biggest of all is Wolf Volcano on Isabela island, while the less active peaks tend to be smaller and older. There are also a number of extinct volcanoes on San Cristóbal and Española, which are some of the oldest and lowest islands in the Galápagos. The scene below shows the volcanoes in order of eruption date.

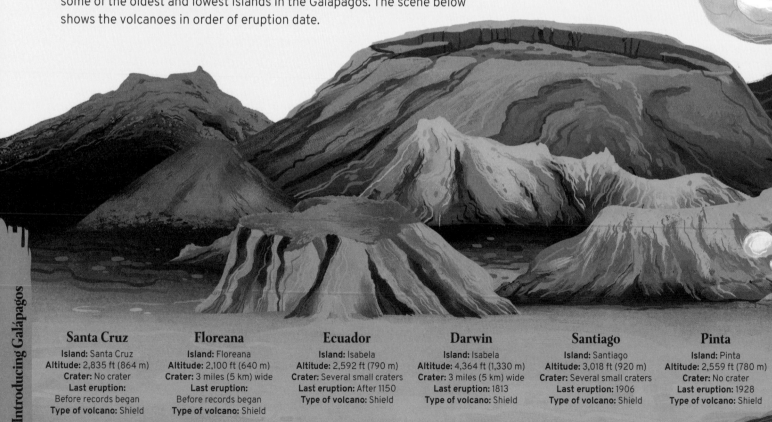

Santa Cruz
Island: Santa Cruz
Altitude: 2,835 ft (864 m)
Crater: No crater
Last eruption: Before records began
Type of volcano: Shield

Floreana
Island: Floreana
Altitude: 2,100 ft (640 m)
Crater: 3 miles (5 km) wide
Last eruption: Before records began
Type of volcano: Shield

Ecuador
Island: Isabela
Altitude: 2,592 ft (790 m)
Crater: Several small craters
Last eruption: After 1150
Type of volcano: Shield

Darwin
Island: Isabela
Altitude: 4,364 ft (1,330 m)
Crater: 3 miles (5 km) wide
Last eruption: 1813
Type of volcano: Shield

Santiago
Island: Santiago
Altitude: 3,018 ft (920 m)
Crater: Several small craters
Last eruption: 1906
Type of volcano: Shield

Pinta
Island: Pinta
Altitude: 2,559 ft (780 m)
Crater: No crater
Last eruption: 1928
Type of volcano: Shield

Shield volcanoes

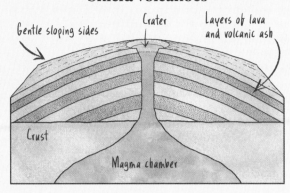

Gentle sloping sides

Crater

Layers of lava and volcanic ash

Crust

Magma chamber

The volcanoes of the Galápagos Islands are shield volcanoes. From sea level, these mountains look like upturned bowls. However, from above they look like medieval warriors' shields, which gives them their name. Shield volcanoes form from fast-flowing lava that spreads out quickly over a wide area during an eruption, before cooling into a layer of solid rock. These layers alternate with layers of volcanic ash and rocks spewed from the crater during violent eruptions, and so volcanoes grow into huge, gently sloping mounds.

Wolf Island

Darwin and Wolf Islands

The two most isolated islands in the Galápagos group are named after the two most significant explorers to visit the islands: Charles Darwin and Theodor Wolf. The islands are crags of rock rising out of the ocean—the last surviving peaks of extinct volcanoes that rise up from the seabed. Darwin Island's coastline is too steep for boats to go ashore. The first humans to set foot on the island arrived by helicopter in 1964.

Darwin Island

Marchena
Island: Marchena
Altitude: 1,125 ft (343 m)
Crater: 4.3 miles (7 km) wide
Last eruption: 1991
Type of volcano: Shield

Alcedo
Island: Isabela
Altitude: 3,707 ft (1,130 m)
Crater: 5 miles (8 km) wide
Last eruption: 1993
Type of volcano: Shield

Cerro Azul
Island: Isabela
Altitude: 5,381 ft (1,640 m)
Crater: 3 miles (5 km) wide
Last eruption: 2008
Type of volcano: Shield

Sierra Negre
Island: Isabela
Altitude: 3,688 ft (1,124 m)
Crater: 5.6 miles (9 km) wide
Last eruption: 2018
Type of volcano: Shield

La Cumbre
Island: Fernandina
Altitude: 4,843 ft (1,476 m)
Crater: 3.7 miles (6 km) wide
Last eruption: 2020
Type of volcano: Shield

Wolf
Island: Isabela
Altitude: 5,600 ft (1,707 m)
Crater: 4.3 miles (7 km) wide
Last eruption: 2022
Type of volcano: Shield

Aa lava

Pronounced "ah-ah," this lava is rather sticky and makes lumps as it flows along. Once it cools, aa covers the land in chunks of spiky black rock.

Pahoehoe lava

Also called rope lava, pahoehoe is runny and smooth when red hot. The upper surface often cools into a rippled rock crust with hot lava flowing underneath.

Lava
and craters

Fumarole

This opening, or vent, on a volcano lets out steam and other—often smelly—gases from deep underground.

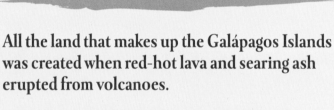

All the land that makes up the Galápagos Islands was created when red-hot lava and searing ash erupted from volcanoes.

Even today, new land can be seen forming around the many active volcanoes on the younger, western islands. However, the older, calmer islands in the east of the archipelago (island chain) still have many signs of their violent, fiery beginnings.

Hornito

This cone-shaped structure forms when lava just below the surface bursts out through an opening and forms a mound. Gas is released from the vent hole at the top of the mound.

Lava tube

A lava tube is a long cave that was once filled with hot lava flowing underneath a crust of cooled lava. When all the lava flowed out, it left a natural tunnel.

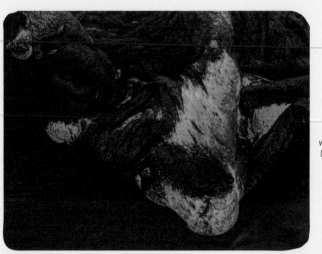

Lava toes

These are formed when hot pahoehoe lava bubbles out of the main flow.

Pit crater

This type of crater forms when the roof of a large lava tube or underground chamber collapses.

Caldera

A caldera is a large crater that appears as the peak of an old volcano begins to crumble back into the empty magma chamber deep underground.

Tuff cone

A tuff cone is a pile of ash formed by an explosive mixture of magma and water.

Driblet cone

Blobs of thick, gooey lava, splattering out of a crater create this small cone of rock.

Volcanic dike

This is a vertical layer of lava rock that has forced its way through older rock layers.

Cinder cone

This common type of volcano is made from fragments of lava called cinders. Cinder cones are often found on the sides of much bigger volcanoes.

Volcanic plug

A volcanic plug is a tower of hard rock that once filled in the vent of a volcano. It's all that remains after softer rocks have been worn away.

Pumice

This soft, lightweight rock forms when lava erupts in water. It cools so quickly that many tiny gas bubbles are trapped inside.

Surrounding oceans

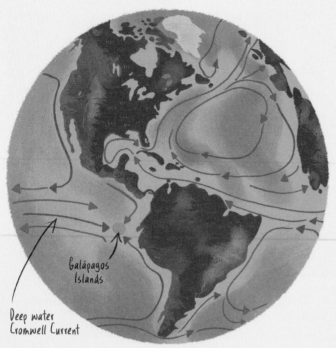

Galápagos Islands

Deep water Cromwell Current

The Galápagos Islands are at a crossroads in the Pacific Ocean, where three ocean currents meet and the upwelling of more nutrient-rich deep waters occurs. Together these help create the favorable conditions for the amazing communities of wildlife for which the islands are world famous.

Upwelling along South America feeds nutrients into the cold Humboldt Current, which has traveled all the way from Antarctica, and carries these rich waters northward. Upwelling along the equator feeds the cold Cromwell Countercurrent, bringing yet more nutrients to the islands. Prevailing winds that drive the warm Panama Current from the northeast pushes water away from the island coastlines and so allows more upwelling to occur.

Hot and cold

The world's oceans are crisscrossed by currents. In general, cold currents flow toward the equator and warm currents flow the other way.

Warm ocean current

Cold ocean current

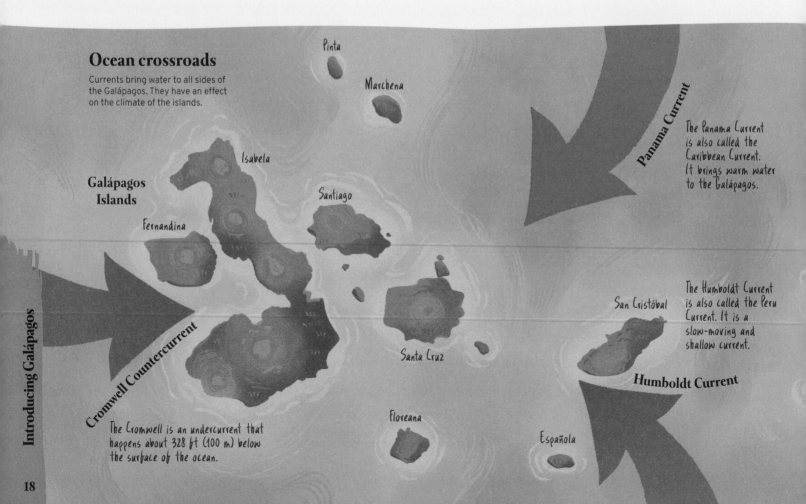

Ocean crossroads

Currents bring water to all sides of the Galápagos. They have an effect on the climate of the islands.

Pinta

Marchena

Isabela

Galápagos Islands

Santiago

Fernandina

Panama Current

The Panama Current is also called the Caribbean Current. It brings warm water to the Galápagos.

San Cristóbal

The Humboldt Current is also called the Peru Current. It is a slow-moving and shallow current.

Cromwell Countercurrent

Santa Cruz

Humboldt Current

The Cromwell is an undercurrent that happens about 328 ft (100 m) below the surface of the ocean.

Floreana

Española

Natural erosion caused Darwin's Arch to collapse.

Darwin's Arch

Ocean currents and wind carved out the rock arch that once stood 141 ft (43 m) above the sea, north of the main Galápagos Islands. Known as Darwin's Arch, the eye-catching structure collapsed in 2021. Seabirds continue to nest on the two rock towers that once supported the arch.

Warm water ⟶ Cold water

Nutrients in the surface water are used by tiny life-forms called plankton.

Nutrient-rich water rises

The Galápagos Islands are fed by the nutrient-rich waters that surround them.

Upwelling

The wind generally blows from east to west across the Galápagos Islands and the surrounding ocean. It pushes the warm surface water away. Cold water from deeper down then upwells, or rises, to take its place, bringing with it nutrients from the ocean depths.

Ecuador

Cold, nutrient-rich water attracts a wealth of ocean life.

Cold water

The ocean at the equator is usually warm, but the Galápagos has a zone of cold water that spreads far out from the islands. Cold water holds more nutrients, and so this cold spot is a haven for wildlife.

Life arrives

The Galápagos Islands formed out of the ocean. They were colonized by animal communities who then helped take over the newer islands.

This gradual process took place in stages. Some species found the Galápagos too inhospitable and perished, while others managed to survive and thrive. First spores such as algae and lichens arrived and germinated on the bare rocks. Then, as soil built up from rock sediment and organic matter, the islands were able to support the first plants such as mosses and grasses. This allowed grazing tortoises to survive as well as birds and predatory snakes. Now, millions of years since the Galápagos first formed, that jumble of life has evolved into the incredible wildlife that makes the islands so special.

Tortoise

Iguana

Rat

Snake

Rafts

Trees that have fallen into rivers and washed out to sea may drift across the ocean for weeks. They are swept along in ocean currents and later washed up on distant shores. The floating logs make rafts for land animals, and it's likely that lizards, tortoises, and snakes all traveled from the mainland to the Galápagos in this way. Tortoises may have floated across on their own, too. Small fish that would normally stay close to shore also reached the islands by following the logs out to sea.

Whales

Seals

Winds

Small songbirds of the Galápagos, such as finches, are not strong enough to fly long distances across oceans. They probably made the journey by being caught up in storm winds that blew them to the islands. Bats and smaller creatures, such as insects and spiders, could also have arrived on the islands by this route. The winds, which mostly blow west from South America, also brought plant seeds and the spores of fungi, ferns, mosses, and lichens.

Bat

Bird

Lichen

Seeds

Winners

The plant life of the Galápagos is dominated by species such as dandelions, grasses, and ferns, which produce tiny, lightweight seeds or spores that are easily spread by the wind. Plants that rely on animals or water to spread their seeds are less common on the islands.

Currents

Sea life would have found the Galápagos Islands by following the many currents that led there, or they may have been swept there by chance during storms. The island chain has everything marine animals need, and so many visitors, including seals and penguins, stayed for good. The islands have become important breeding grounds for sea turtles and seabirds, while whales, dolphins, and sharks frequently visit to feed in the fertile waters that surround the islands.

Penguin

Losers

Large mammals and frogs are the two groups of animals that never made it to the Galápagos Islands by natural means. Log rafts cannot hold big mammals, such as jaguars or bears. Only small mammals, such as rats and bats, have made the journey. Frogs and other amphibians are killed by saltwater and wouldn't survive an ocean crossing.

Island climate and seasons

The Galápagos Islands are warm and sunny all year round. Instead of the four seasons experienced in cooler parts of the world, the islands have just two seasons: wet and dry.

The first half of the year is the wet season. This is the warmest period, with temperatures reaching around 82°F (28°C). The temperature of the sea increases, too, and its waters evaporate to form thick clouds that create rainstorms over the islands. The cloud cover also helps to trap the hot air closer to land. The second half of the year is the dry season. Although, it isn't completely dry since there is a cool fine drizzle brought in by the strengthening Humboldt current, which keeps the higher humid zones wet. The air and sea cool, with some days only reaching 70°F (21°C). The winds blowing in from South America get stronger, but the cooler air has fewer clouds and so the weather stays dry. The clear skies allow heat to escape as soon as the sun goes down.

Floreana Island during the wet season.

The seasons

In the Galápagos, the two seasons are very different. The wet season has warm waters and gentle winds, while the dry season has cooler waters and stronger winds.

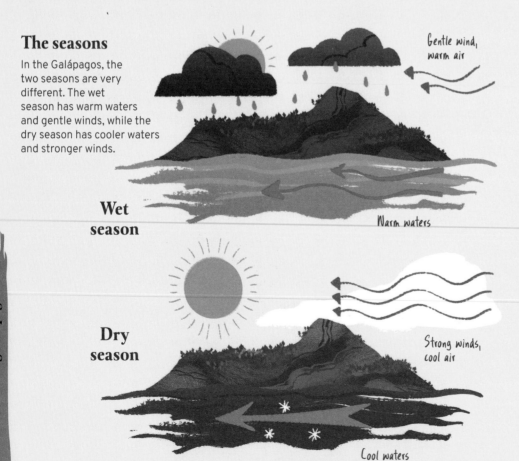

Gentle wind, warm air

Wet season

Warm waters

Dry season

Strong winds, cool air

Cool waters

Warm parts of the Pacific Ocean.

El Niño

Every few years, the Pacific Ocean sees a big shift in its climate. The change is called El Niño, which means "The Boy" in Spanish. It refers to the Baby Jesus because one of its effects is warmer weather in South America at Christmas. El Niño happens when the colder Humboldt current coming up from the south weakens, which helps warmer Pacific waters coming from the west to dominate. This weakens currents that meet at the Galápagos Islands, resulting in the water around the islands becoming warmer. The impact of El Niño can be seen around the world. On the Galápagos Islands, it reduces the amount of food available for both sea life and land animals.

Lean times

El Niño changes the way water moves around the Galápagos Islands, and the upwelling of nutrient-rich water from the deep seabed stops. This means the water around the islands runs out of the nutrients that sea life needs to survive. Everything begins to starve, including animals on the shore, such as iguanas and sea lions. However, life soon recovers when the currents shift back and the cold water returns.

Cormorant Point on Floreana Island during the El Niño dry season.

Marine iguana skeleton

23

The voyage of the *Beagle*

The Galápagos Islands are world famous today thanks to Charles Darwin. He was the English scientist who came up with the theory of evolution, which explains how plants and animals can change over time.

Darwin visited the islands in 1835 aboard HMS *Beagle*, a British research ship. He joined the crew not as an official scientist, but as a paying passenger on board to keep the captain company for the five-year expedition. After returning to England, Darwin wrote about what he saw on the long adventure in a book called *The Voyage of the Beagle*. The many observations he made led him to think about how life on Earth evolves.

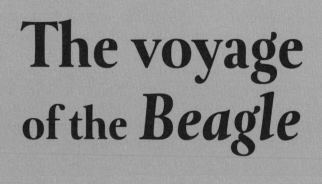

Canary Islands

Galápagos Islands

Patagonia

Falkland Islands

→ Departing journey
→ Return journey

The long journey

The *Beagle*'s voyage took it around the world, crossing the Atlantic Ocean and sailing on to visit many of the Pacific islands and Australia. Darwin was only twenty-two years old when the ship set off from England. He had just finished studying science at college and was thinking about becoming a priest. His main interests were geology (study of rocks and the Earth) and wildlife, and he collected many specimens during the long voyage.

Canary Islands

At the Canary Islands, in the Atlantic Ocean, Darwin used a net with very small holes to collect tiny creatures floating in the seawater. He was amazed by how many organisms—now known as plankton—were in the net.

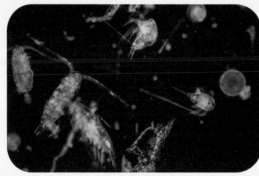

The *Beagle*

The *Beagle* was built as a warship, but it was never used for fighting. Instead, it was equipped to explore the world's seas, with a crew of around seventy, who made detailed maps and tracked the direction of ocean currents. Darwin traveled on the ship's second of three around-the-world voyages that explored the Southern Hemisphere.

Patagonia

While ashore in Patagonia (southern South America), Darwin found the fossil skull of a megatherium. This giant sloth grew to 20 ft (6 m) long—unlike anything that lives in South America today.

Falkland Islands

Darwin saw a large canine species, known as the Falkland Islands wolf, while on these South Atlantic islands. He rightly predicted that the canine would become extinct because the settlers killed so many of them. It died out in 1876.

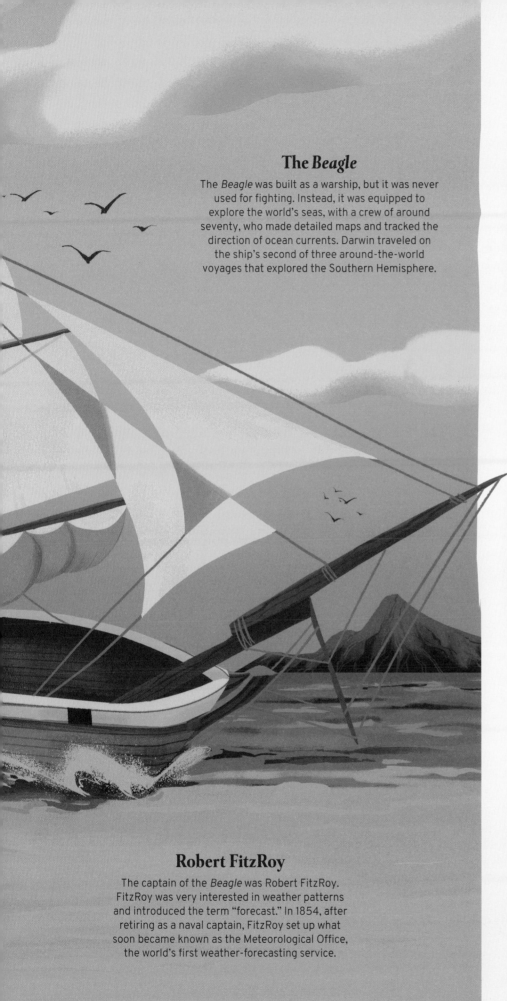

Robert FitzRoy

The captain of the *Beagle* was Robert FitzRoy. FitzRoy was very interested in weather patterns and introduced the term "forecast." In 1854, after retiring as a naval captain, FitzRoy set up what soon became known as the Meteorological Office, the world's first weather-forecasting service.

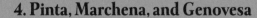

Darwin

Wolf

6. Wolf and Darwin

The *Beagle* sailed back to Santiago Island, via Española (then called Hood Island), to pick up Darwin and the other campers. The ship was almost ready to leave the Galápagos. It finished its survey by heading northwest to Wenman and Culpepper. Today, Wenman is called Wolf Island, after the German naturalist Theodor Wolf, who explored the Galápagos around fifty years after Darwin. Culpepper Island is now called Darwin, after Charles Darwin.

4. Pinta, Marchena, and Genovesa

After leaving Isabela, the *Beagle*'s captain, Robert FitzRoy, turned the ship north to take a look at Abingdon, Bindloe, and Tower islands—today known as Pinta, Marchena, and Genovesa. Over the next four days, he struggled against the wind and currents and was unable to find a place to get ashore on any of these small islands. Running out of drinking water, the *Beagle* headed back south to the next island.

Pinta

Marchena   Genovesa

Setting up camp

Darwin and Bynoe—helped by their two servants—set up a tent in a sheltered valley near Buccaneer Cove on Santiago. They had a local guide, who was visiting the island to hunt tortoises. He took Darwin inland into the highlands, where the giant tortoises gathered around a watering hole. Before leaving, Darwin captured a baby Santiago tortoise to keep as a pet aboard the *Beagle*. The tortoise died before reaching England.

Santiago

Fernandina

Santa Cruz

Isabela

Floreana

3. Isabela

The next stop was Albermarle Island, now known as Isabela. The ship spent six days moving around this island, by far the largest in the archipelago. This volcanic island is where Darwin first noted seeing finches. Here Darwin also made his first close observation of marine iguanas diving into the sea to feed. He assumed that these lizards were hunting for fish, but later found that they ate algae.

Surveying the islands

The discoveries made by Darwin in the Galápagos overshadow the other work carried out by the crew of the *Beagle*. The main reason the ship visited the islands was to make a map of the islands' coastlines, volcanoes, and other major landmarks. Much of this work was done by survey parties. Unlike Darwin, these teams visited every island in the archipelago.

5. Santiago

The *Beagle* then moved on to James, or Santiago, Island. The crew couldn't find a source of fresh water on this island, so they returned to San Cristóbal to resupply. Darwin and the ship's doctor, Benjamin Bynoe, stayed behind and managed to find fresh water from a spring. They set up camp at Buccaneer Cove and spent nine days exploring and collecting specimens, such as finches. Later, these were classified by ornithologist John Gould and used to support Darwin's theory of evolution.

Darwin at the Galápagos

The HMS *Beagle*—with Charles Darwin on board—arrived at the Galápagos Islands on September 15, 1835. The ship toured the islands for a little more than a month, and on October 20, 1835, it set off for Tahiti in the center of the Pacific.

The main job of the *Beagle*'s crew was to make detailed maps of the islands. Survey parties—the men drawing up the maps—toured the islands in small boats, but Darwin mostly traveled around the islands aboard the *Beagle* itself. He spent only a few hours on most islands, watching the wildlife, making records of the landscape, and collecting specimens of plants, animals, and rocks.

San Cristóbal

añola

1. San Cristóbal

The *Beagle* arrived first on San Cristóbal, which the British sailors knew as Chatham Island back then. Darwin did not come ashore for three days while the *Beagle* moved around the island and anchored in several bays. Once on land, he noticed how tame the birds were and made notes about the rocky lava landscape and its craters. It was here that Darwin saw giant tortoises for the first time, when they were being captured by the ship's crew as a source of food.

2. Floreana

The next island—which Darwin knew as Charles Island—was much greener than the first. Here, the explorers met Nicholas Lawson, a prison governor, who gave them a tour. Lawson explained that the giant tortoises from each island all had differently shaped shells. Sadly, these tortoises became extinct in 1846. The Floreana mockingbird is extinct on Floreana, but is found on two tiny islets close by. A year later, Darwin compared the differences between the mockingbirds on Floreana and San Cristóbal.

Follow HMS *Beagle* on its journey around the Galápagos Islands

A story of evolution

One of the most important observations made by Charles Darwin on his visit to the Galápagos Islands was how each island had its own species of plants and animals.

For example, the tortoises on one island were slightly different from those living on another. Darwin began thinking about how this could be. He pondered the problem for many years and came up with the theory of evolution by natural selection. Darwin told the world about evolution in his 1859 book: *On the Origin of Species.*

Evolving in isolation

The evolution of many of the species in the Galápagos has been driven by the fact that they are living in isolation. The islands' species do not have the same community of predators and other competitors that surround their relatives on the mainland. For example, the flightless cormorant's ancestors flew to the Galápagos Islands. However, on the islands, the birds did not use their wings because they had no need to fly away from predators, and they evolved to be flightless.

Natural selection

Darwin's theory is summed up by the phrase "the survival of the fittest." No two animals in a population are the same; there is always variation between them. This variation means some animals have characteristics that make them better suited than others to thrive in one place. This is what Darwin means by being "fit." The "unfit" animals don't have these helpful characteristics so can't compete for food and are more likely to die. The fit ones survive more easily and have many offspring. Nature has selected them, and so their useful characteristics become more common. The group of animals has therefore changed, or evolved.

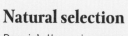

Ancestors

A population of finches of the same species are blown off course and arrive on an island in the Galápagos. They are thin-beaked birds best suited to eating small insects. However, there are small inherited differences in the exact shape and size of the beaks within this population.

Many generations later

On the island, the main food supply is hard seeds, and the finches with thicker beaks and a stronger bite can crack the seeds and get more food. These birds are more likely to survive to breed and pass on the thick-beaked characteristic. Over many generations and millions of years, this natural selection produces a population of birds with very big, thick beaks.

Evolving species

One island species

Giant tortoises with domed shells from South America colonize a steep-sided Galápagos island and survive by grazing on grass that grows on the moist hillsides.

Moving home

The population splits up as some of the tortoises make their way to another island. However, this island is flatter and drier—with tall cacti and very little grass.

Natural selection

Over many generations on the flat island, tortoises born with higher-fronted shells find they can reach up to eat cactus pads. They survive better than the tortoises with domed shells, which have to make do with the sparse grass on the ground. The high-fronted, or "saddleback," shells are naturally selected and the domed ones begin to disappear.

Two island species

Millions of years later, the saddleback tortoises living on the dry, flat island are now so different from the domed tortoises on the wetter, hilly island that the two kinds could no longer interbreed. They are now two separate species.

Reptiles are very quiet. The loudest reptilian sound on the Galápagos is the moo-like mating call of the giant tortoise!

Reptiles

The Galápagos Islands are one of the few places on Earth where the biggest animals are reptiles. In most other places, mammals take that prize. The islands are generally hot and dry—conditions that suit cold-blooded reptiles, which need to warm up in the sunshine each morning. Their scaly and leathery skin also made reptiles better suited than mammals to surviving the long ocean crossing to the islands. Every kind of reptile on the Galápagos is descended from an animal that survived for weeks at sea without food and water.

Galápagos land iguana on the caldera floor of La Cumbre volcano, Fernandina Island, Galápagos.

31

Marine iguana

Marine iguanas have evolved to make a life on the rough rocks that were created when lava flows hit the cold ocean. Their sharp teeth and blunt noses allow them to eat algae growing on rocks.

Giant tortoise

Inland and uphill from the coast, the islands have areas with shrublands, grasslands, and deciduous forests. This is an ideal habitat for plant-eating reptiles, such as giant tortoises.

Reptiles

Large eyes for good night vision.

The Galápagos Islands are home to most kinds of reptiles found in other parts of the world. There are tortoises and sea turtles, snakes, and lizards, such as iguanas and geckos. Crocodiles are the only major kind of reptile not seen on the islands.

Although the different reptiles on the islands look and live in very different ways, they all share a set of basic characteristics. They have skin covered in scales coated with a water-resistant substance called keratin. They are all cold-blooded, which means their body temperature varies with the environment. And while a few reptiles farther afield give birth to their young, the reptiles on the Galápagos all lay eggs.

Five species of geckos live on the Galápagos Islands. This leaf-toed gecko is found nowhere else in the world.

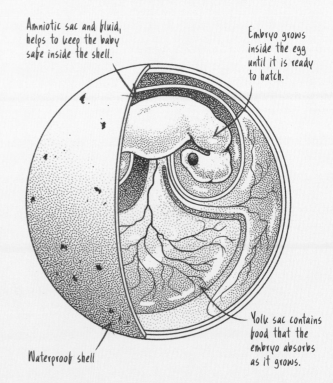

Lava lizard

Small scurrying lava lizards are widespread across the islands. They live in the warm lowland regions nearer the shoreline and can be seen warming up in the sun on dark rocks.

Racer snakes

Beaches are home to many of the islands' racer snakes. They prey upon geckos, lava lizards, rats, mice, insects, bird hatchlings, and marine iguanas.

The long tail may break off during a fight, to startle the attacker.

Geckos store fat in their tails, to use when food is scarce.

Pads on the toes have tiny hairs for gripping any surface.

Shell protection

Reptiles are able to breed in dry places thanks to the shells around their eggs. The shell is waterproof so the liquid egg white and yolk, which feeds the baby as it grows, does not dry out. However, the shell does let gases in and out, so the baby reptile can breathe inside.

Amniotic sac and fluid, helps to keep the baby safe inside the shell.

Embryo grows inside the egg until it is ready to hatch.

Waterproof shell

Yolk sac contains food that the embryo absorbs as it grows.

Marine iguanas

Marine iguanas vary greatly in size—between 5 in (12 cm) and 61 in (156 cm) long from nose to tip of the tail.

The marine iguana is the only lizard in the world that collects all its food from the ocean. Like all reptiles, this iguana is cold-blooded. This means it's most active when it's warm, and sluggish when it's cold. For this reason, it can't stay in the chilly waters around the Galápagos for too long when it's feeding.

A smaller iguana, usually young or female, feeds on algae on the exposed rocks at the water's edge, while the larger, male iguana dives down to graze on algae. It can dive 49 ft (15 m) below the surface and can stay underwater for around twenty minutes. When its strength begins to fade, it clambers back up the rocks to warm up in the sun. The sun's heat also helps the lizard digest its food, and gives it the energy it needs for its next feed.

There is just one species of marine iguana. Even though these lizards don't tend to travel between the islands, they have managed to spread across the Galápagos. Scientists studying the different populations have split marine iguanas into at least eleven distinct subspecies.

Too much salt!

Salt gland

Salty snot

A diet of just algae means that marine iguanas eat a lot of salt. Too much salt in the body is harmful, so it needs to be excreted, or gotten rid of. The marine iguana has special glands inside its nose to help it. They remove salt from the blood, and the iguana then sneezes it out as salty snot!

The crest helps the iguana remain stable in rough currents underwater. It also impresses mates and scares off rivals.

Marine iguanas have short, tripod-shaped teeth to help them to scrape algae from rocks.

Male iguanas use the chemicals in their food to produce colorful patterns on their skin to attract mates.

The hooked claws are useful for climbing over rocks, on land and underwater.

Diving, swimming, and grazing

A larger iguana dives into the sea from volcanic rocks. It takes a deep breath since it can't breathe underwater.

Its short legs fold out of the way against the sides of its body, and the iguana uses its long, paddle-shaped tail to swim down to the seabed.

The iguana uses its long, sturdy claws to cling to the rocks as it bites off the algae. Its short, flat nose is suited to grazing on the rocks.

Hot lava and cold water

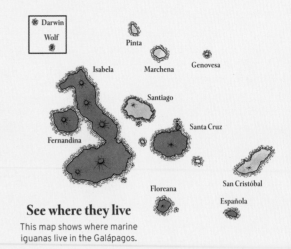

See where they live
This map shows where marine iguanas live in the Galápagos.

The male marine iguana spends its time moving between two very different habitats.

One moment, the male marine iguana is basking on the rocky shore, where the sunshine bakes the dark lava rocks. The next, it's diving into chilly water, in search of its food—algae. The female and juvenile marine iguanas look for food on the intertidal rocks. The marine iguana is cold blooded, which means it can't control its body temperature. To survive, this lizard behaves in different ways to warm up and cool down.

The snout is often covered in a crust of salt crystals that have been sneezed out of the nose.

Managing body temperature
After climbing out of the chilly water, the lizards' wet skin is darker than when it's dry. Dark colors absorb heat easily, so the iguana dries out and warms up fast in the sun's rays.

Sky-pointing
When marine iguanas get too hot, they stand tall on their front legs, so their heads are pointing straight up. This sky-pointing position reduces the amount of hot sunshine that hits the body.

Changing bodies

In the breeding season, the big male iguanas develop bright coloring to attract females. The chemicals that produce the vibrant patterns come from the algae the lizards eat, and the patterns and colors vary from island to island. The biggest and brightest iguanas often fight for the female iguanas by butting heads.

Shrinking lizards

During El Niño periods, there's less food around for the iguanas. These long-bodied lizards have a remarkable tactic for coping. They absorb nutrients from their own bones and muscles to power their bodies. This causes the iguanas to become both thinner and shorter. They grow back to their full size when food becomes plentiful again.

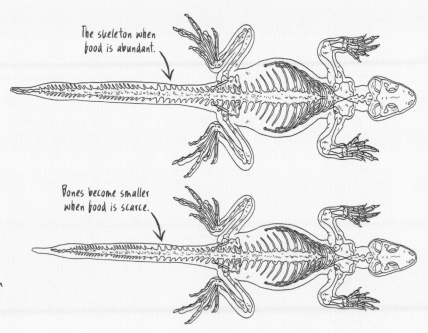

The skeleton when food is abundant.

Bones become smaller when food is scarce.

The sky-pointing position stops marine iguanas from overheating in the hot, midday sunshine.

Cold ⟶ Hot

Night-time huddle

As night falls, the heat in the rocks starts to leak back out into the air. The marine iguanas huddle together as it gets colder, sharing their body heat while they sleep through the night.

See where they live

This map shows where land iguanas live in the Galápagos.

Darwin
Wolf
Pinta
Isabela
Marchena
Genovesa
Santiago
Santa Cruz
Fernandina
Floreana
San Cristóbal
Española

Fight!

Land iguanas spend most of their time alone. They try to scare off other iguanas they meet by gaping their mouth open to reveal their teeth and pale pink gums. If that doesn't work, the rivals try to bite each other's necks to show who's boss.

Spines protect the back of the iguana's neck and the top of its head.

Bad review

Charles Darwin was not impressed by the land iguanas he encountered on the islands. He described them as "ugly animals... with a stupid appearance." He even cut a few open to find out what they ate.

Many of the scales are rough and pointed.

Land iguanas

This lumbering, scaly monster is the largest lizard living on the Galápagos. It's a close relative of the marine iguana but around twice its size when fully grown, sometimes reaching 5 ft (1.5 m) long and weighing 29 lb (13 kg).

There are three species of Galápagos land iguanas. The most common one is spread across all the larger islands. A slightly smaller species with paler skin lives on Santa Fé, a small island near Santa Cruz. The third species, the pink iguana, is only found high on the slopes of Wolf Volcano on Isabela. Adult land iguanas are plant eaters. However, when they are young, they eat a wider range of foods, including beetles, centipedes, and even chicks. Like all reptiles, land iguanas are cold-blooded, and they can often be seen sunbathing in the morning. By the middle of the day, however, it's usually too hot for them, so they rest in the shade.

Pink lizard

There are only around one hundred individuals of the pink land iguana, which lives in a little-visited part of Isabela. This iguana was first spotted in 1986, and scientists only proved that it was a separate species in 2009!

Pink land iguanas live in an area of just 10 sq miles (25 sq km).

Volcanic nursery

Female land iguanas on Fernandina need a warm place to bury their eggs, so they climb to the edge of the crater of the island's volcano, La Cumbre.

The iguanas then scramble into the active crater, finding a way down the steep, unstable sides, while trying to avoid falling rocks.

When they reach the floor of the crater, they lay their eggs in the warm, soft ash. When the baby iguanas hatch, they have to climb all the way out!

Española lava lizard (male)

Pinzón lava lizard (female)

Lava lizards

Santiago lava lizard (female)

These striking lizards are among the most widespread reptiles of the Galápagos Islands. As their name suggests, they forage for food on the rough rocks that cover the islands. They eat whatever they can find, from maggots and ants to flowers and leaves.

There are ten species of lava lizards living on the Galápagos. All the species belong to the genus *Microlophus*. The Galápagos lava lizard (*M. albemarlensis*) is the most widespread. Other species are confined to one island each, including the Pinzón lava lizard (*M. duncanensis*), found only on tiny Pinzón Island. The different species can be told apart by their colorful markings.

San Cristóbal lava lizard (male)

Santa Cruz lava lizard (female)

Iguana cousins

The lava lizards are relatives of the Galápagos iguanas, although they evolved to be much smaller—only around 6 in (15 cm) from nose to tail tip. They share the same habitats as their iguana cousins, and often climb onto their backs to catch flies and other insects.

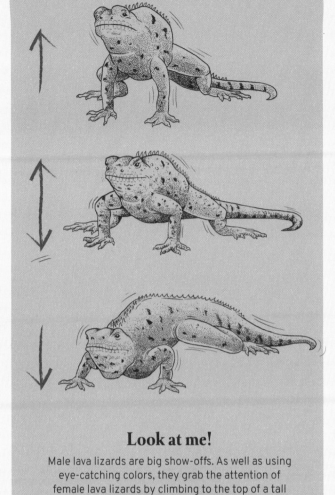

Galápagos lava lizard (female)

Look at me!

Male lava lizards are big show-offs. As well as using eye-catching colors, they grab the attention of female lava lizards by climbing to the top of a tall rock and performing push-ups!

Male and female

It's easy to tell a female lava lizard from a male. She's around three-quarters his length and has smoother skin. The male lava lizard also has much rougher scales, and a crest of spines along the back of its neck.

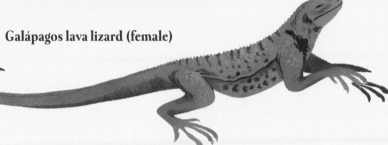

Santa Fé lava lizard (male)

Floreana lava lizard (male)

Pinta lava lizard (female)

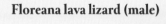

Racer snakes

As their name suggests, racer snakes use speed to catch food. They are ambushers that slither out and snatch prey in a flash. The Galápagos Islands are home to nine species of racer snakes. They're all very slender and rarely grow longer than 3.3 ft (1 m). Different species live on different islands.

Racer snakes live in the dry areas close to the shoreline, in dry shrublands and grasslands, in deciduous forests, in gardens, and sometimes (depending upon the island) bare volcanic rock. They prey on small lizards, insects, and chicks.

Scales colored gray and brown match the sandy habitat.

Small, rounded head

Run for your life

Racer snakes are difficult to spot because they usually hide among the rocks. However, when prey appears—such as a newly hatched baby iguana—racers will soon slither out into the open and give chase. Their long bodies slide easily over the sand, while the lizard's little feet struggle to run fast enough.

Whiplike tail

Spots, stripes, and speckles blend in with rough ground.

The Fernandina racer is the only land snake in the world to catch fish from rock pools.

Long, slender body

Killer tactics

Racer snakes are harmless to humans, but they're expert killers when they catch prey. First of all, the snake grabs its victim in its powerful jaws.

The snake injects a weak venom through its fangs into the prey to stop it from struggling. The predator then wraps its coils around the victim, steadily squeezing it until it stops breathing.

When the prey is dead, the snake releases its grip and begins to swallow it. The snake cannot bite off chunks of food, so it opens its mouth wide and swallows the animal whole, and always headfirst.

Giant tortoises

See where they live
The giant tortoises live on the islands colored in white.

Darwin
Wolf
Pinta
Marchena
Genovesa
Isabela
Santiago
Fernandina
Santa Cruz
Floreana
San Cristóbal
Española

The upper part of the shell is called the carapace.

The largest and most famous animals living on the Galápagos Islands are the giant tortoises. These tank-like reptiles leave a deep impression on any visitor. The name of the islands even comes from an old Spanish word for "tortoise."

It's thought the first giant tortoises arrived from South America—washed out to sea on a floating raft of trees—around three million years ago. They might have also floated on their own. Since then, that original species has evolved into many new species that are now spread across the islands.

The term "giant" is very fitting for these animals. A pet tortoise might easily sit on your hand, but an adult Galápagos tortoise is around 5 ft (1.5 m) long and would fill most of your bed! It might even break it, too, since the biggest adults weigh 550 lb (250 kg)—that's three times as much as an adult man. Although huge, the tortoises are harmless creatures, and very slow— they take twenty minutes to walk 330 ft (100 m).

The mouth is toothless but has a sharp jawbone.

The neck can curl to pull the head into the shell.

Dry, scaly skin

The front feet have five claws.

An average adult giant tortoise stands at 2 ft 8 in (82 cm) tall.

The expected average height of a woman in the UK is 5 ft 4 in (163 cm).

Hatchlings

A female giant tortoise lays around a dozen round eggs—each around the size of a tennis ball—in a hole dug into soft ground. This nest is warmed by the sun, and the babies hatch after around four months and dig themselves out. The sex of the baby is decided by its position in the nest. The eggs in the deeper and cooler parts develop into males, while the eggs in the warmer parts near the surface become female tortoises.

The shell is made from bone plates covered in keratin.

Giant tortoises spend around sixteen hours each day sleeping.

Age-old creatures

Giant tortoises are one of the longest-living land animals. It's quite normal for these mighty plant munchers to live for more than a hundred years, and there are records of them living much longer. One tortoise named Harriet (above)—taken from the Galápagos to Australia—was around 176 years old when she died in 2006. As a young tortoise, she would have been on the Galápagos when Charles Darwin visited in 1885, although he didn't set foot on her island, Santa Cruz.

The flat lower part of the shell is called the plastron.

The back feet have four claws.

Shell shapes
and habitats

Saddleback shell

The tortoises on Española have particularly obvious saddleback shells, while the western Santa Cruz tortoises have high domes on their backs.

The shells of the giant tortoises on the Galápagos come in two main shapes: domed and saddleback. A domed shell is the typical tortoise-shell shape, while a saddleback shell is shaped a lot like a fancy horse saddle used long ago.

Domed shell

Evolution has changed the upper part of the shell, or carapace, to suit the habitat where each species lives. Saddleback shells let tortoises lift their heads high to reach leaves or cactus pads on tall plants. Domed shells don't allow this, so instead the animals bend their heads downward to eat low-growing plants, such as grasses.

Dry and high

The saddleback tortoises live on low-lying islands or regions where the weather is often hot and dry. The plants there are tall bushes and cacti, so the tortoises need to be able to reach food above their heads.

The shell is curved up behind the neck so the tortoise can stretch its head upward.

Saddleback tortoises have longer necks and legs to reach up into tall plants.

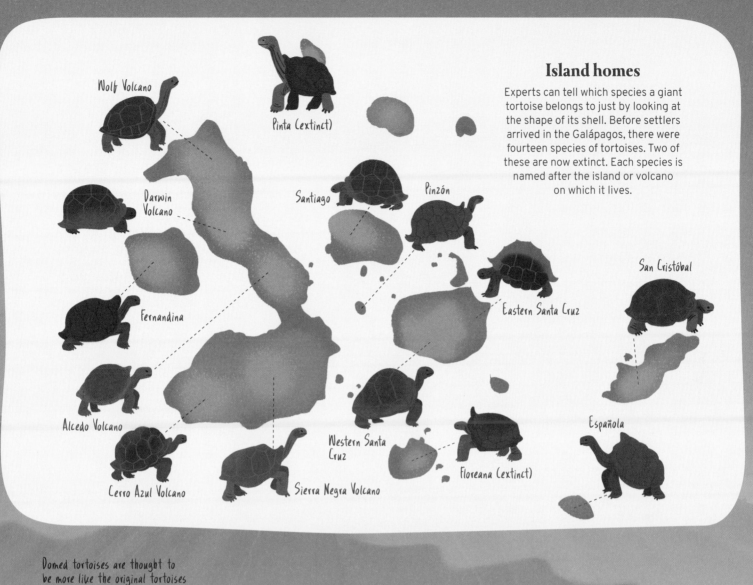

Island homes

Experts can tell which species a giant tortoise belongs to just by looking at the shape of its shell. Before settlers arrived in the Galápagos, there were fourteen species of tortoises. Two of these are now extinct. Each species is named after the island or volcano on which it lives.

Wolf Volcano

Pinta (extinct)

Darwin Volcano

Santiago

Pinzón

San Cristóbal

Fernandina

Eastern Santa Cruz

Alcedo Volcano

Western Santa Cruz

Española

Cerro Azul Volcano

Sierra Negra Volcano

Floreana (extinct)

Domed tortoises are thought to be more like the original tortoises that reached the islands.

Head down

Domed tortoises live on islands with lush highland areas. There, the weather is often damp, and grasses and herbs grow low to the ground, within easy reach.

Domed tortoises have shorter necks.

Lonesome George

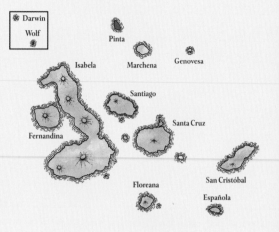

Darwin
Wolf
Pinta
Isabela
Marchena
Genovesa
Santiago
Santa Cruz
Fernandina
Floreana
San Cristóbal
Española

George was once the most famous tortoise in the world, but he was very lonesome (lonely). For at least forty years, he had been one of a kind—the last of the Pinta Island tortoises. This species of giant tortoises was thought to have been wiped out completely in the 1950s, when goats were released on Pinta Island. They ate nearly all the shrubs and grasses, outcompeting the tortoises.

However, George was found alive among the rocks on Pinta in 1971. After searching high and low, scientists couldn't find any other tortoises on the small island. There were no mates for Lonesome George, and the Pinta Island tortoise became extinct when he died in 2012.

Long neck for reaching tall shrubs

The rarest animal in the world
Lonesome George was already around sixty years old when he was found in the wild, but he still had many years to live. After his discovery, he was moved to a safe home at the Charles Darwin Research Station on Santa Cruz Island. Here, he became a global symbol of the conservation needed to protect the native species of the Galápagos.

Lonesome George could survive for six months without food or water.

Reptiles

48

Breeding attempts

At the research station, George lived with females from other closely related giant tortoise species. Scientists hoped George would mate with the females and produce hybrid tortoises similar to the Pinta Island species. Although some eggs were laid, no baby tortoises ever hatched.

George had been alone for such a long time that he needed help learning how to be around other tortoises.

Possible relatives

Very close relatives of George have been found living on the slopes of Wolf Volcano on Isabela Island. Pinta tortoises were probably put here long ago by sailors, who often carried live tortoises on their ships as a source of food. These Pinta tortoises interbred with the Wolf Volcano species. Scientists are now searching for any of the original Pinta tortoises that might still be alive on Isabela.

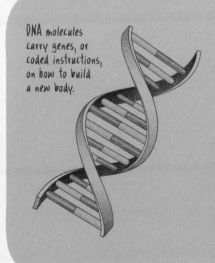

DNA molecules carry genes, or coded instructions, on how to build a new body.

Genetic Technology

Before he died, George's genome—the full set of his DNA—was decoded. This showed that George shared 90 percent of his genes with the tortoise species from eastern Santa Cruz. By studying these genes, scientists can understand more about how giant tortoises live—and perhaps why they can live so long. All this information is useful for helping to figure out how best to conserve the populations of giant tortoises that still survive on the Galápagos Islands.

A young female tortoise with Pinta island ancestry.

There are around fifty species of birds living in the Galápagos Islands, and around half of them are found nowhere else in the world.

Birds

The Galápagos Islands are full of birds wherever you look—from the surrounding ocean and rocky shoreline to the dry shrubland, forest, and lush highland slopes. Thanks to their power of flight, birds were better suited to finding their way to the islands than other land animals. And they keep coming! Recently, cattle egrets arrived here, and it looks like they will stay. The birds that came to the Galápagos long before the egrets have since been shaped by evolution into separate species that live in every nook and cranny of these amazing islands.

Galápagos hawk in flight above the Alcedo Volcano, Isabela Island, Galápagos.

Birds of prey have long, wide wings.

Seabirds have long, narrow wings.

Songbirds have wings with rounded ends.

Ducks have curved wings.

Birds

Wing shapes

The shape of a bird's wings shows you how it flies. Long, wide wings are suited to slow flight and steep swoops, whereas long, narrow wings are for gliding long distances. Wings with rounded ends are used for making short flights with sharp turns, and wings with curved edges are for flying fast.

The Galápagos is a haven for bird lovers, who are drawn to these remote islands in the Pacific from all over the world. They come to see the rare and unique birds living in the wide variety of habitats found on the islands.

On one day, birdwatchers might marvel at vast seabird colonies, containing thousands of screeching birds. The following day, they might seek out tiny songbirds farther inland and witness their incredible behavior. The islands' birds always put on a good show. They are famous for not being frightened away by human observers—but visitors shouldn't get too close or touch them.

Galápagos mockingbird

The islands are home to four species of mockingbirds, which live in small flocks. Although mockingbirds are so named because they imitate the calls of other species, the Galápagos species are not known to do this.

American flamingo

Mostly found in the Caribbean, small flocks of these large pink birds live in the salty lagoons of the Galápagos. Flamingos have sieve-like beaks, which they use to sift food from the muddy water.

Magnificent frigatebird

The Galápagos Islands are one of the few places in the Pacific where the magnificent frigatebird breeds. This seabird can spend many weeks in flight without needing to land. It soars above the waves, snatching fish from the surface—and from other seabirds, too!

Hooked beak for snatching fish

Long, forked tail

Male's red throat pouch attracts mates.

Wings can be up to 7.5 ft (2.3 m) across.

The magnificent frigatebird has the lightest skeleton for a bird of its size.

Cormorant

This diving shorebird is so well adapted to catching fish underwater that its wings are no longer capable of flight. Instead the big bird hops along the rocky shore, looking into the water for its next meal.

Galápagos hawk

The largest hunting bird on the islands, the Galápagos hawk can be seen searching for prey in all habitats. With only a small patch of land to call home, the hawk eats a wide range of foods from centipedes to snakes.

Large tree finch

This bird uses its strong, curved beak for grasping large insects, such as beetles.

Medium tree finch

The beak of this finch is more pointed than that of its larger relative and used for snatching smaller prey.

Small tree finch

This little bird uses its pointed beak to grab insects. It also eats fruit, seeds, and nectar.

Food: mostly fruit

Food: mostly insects

TREE FINCHES

Five species of Darwin's finches make their home in trees, where they feed on the insects and other invertebrates that crawl around the branches. Each finch targets a different kind of insect prey.

Vegetarian finch

One of the few kinds of mostly leaf-eating birds, this finch also eats buds, flowers, and fruit. It has a parrot-like beak.

Cocos finch

Related to the Galápagos finches, this bird lives on Cocos Island, north of the Galápagos. It eats fruit, nectar, insects, and seeds. It has a downward-curving beak.

Food: mostly leaves

Food: mostly insects

Warbler finch

The smallest of Darwin's finches, this bird has a slender, pointed beak for grabbing insects.

Food: mostly insects

Darwin's finches

There are many species of finches in the Galápagos. The birds are known as Darwin's finches because Charles Darwin took a great interest in them.

Darwin made detailed drawings of the finches' different beak shapes. He wanted to understand how the closely related species came to have a wide range of beak shapes and sizes, and live in different ways across the Galápagos Islands. The evidence from the finches' beaks helped Darwin figure out his famous theory of evolution. The theory explains how they all descended from a flock of ancestors that arrived from tropical America. They evolved into many different species with beaks suited to different diets—probably within a million years.

Sharp-beaked ground finch

This finch eats a variety of foods—including insects, flowers, leaves, and cactus pulp.

ANCESTRAL FINCH

No one knows exactly what the ancestral bird was like, but it was probably similar to a group of seed-eating finches called grassquits that are today found in open habitats of South America—including the Andes Mountains.

Woodpecker finch

This insectivore has a long beak for a finch and can use tools (right). It also eats fruit and seeds.

Learning skills

Animals that use tools are very smart. One of Darwin's finches—the woodpecker finch—does exactly this. It grips a small twig in its beak and uses it to dig out insects, especially the larvae (grubs) from crevices in trees. Young woodpecker finches learn the skill by watching older birds.

Mangrove finch

Found only in swamp forests on the northwestern coast of Isabela, this finch uses its delicate beak to pick off insects on tree and shrub bark.

Common cactus finch

This bird has a long, pointed beak. It is a specialized feeder of prickly pear cactus seeds. It also eats cactus flowers and insects. It helps to spread the plant's pollen.

GROUND FINCHES

These finches search for seeds that have fallen to the ground from trees and shrubs. This way of feeding is typical of many finches around the world.

Food: mostly seeds

Food: insects and blood

Española cactus finch

A close relative of the common cactus finch, this bird has a stout beak and feeds mostly on prickly pear seeds.

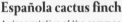

Small ground finch

Found across the Galápagos, this little bird eats seeds, buds, and fruit. It also uses its short, pointed beak to catch insects.

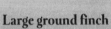

Large ground finch

The largest of Darwin's finches, this bird has a big beak suited to crushing large seeds. It lives in the dry lowland areas of the main islands.

Vampire ground finch

Found only on Wolf and Darwin Islands, this bird uses its sharp beak to peck at the feet of nesting boobies and then drinks their blood!

Medium ground finch

As well as seeds, this sturdy-beaked bird also eats the leaves of low-growing shrubs.

Genovesa ground finch

This close relative of the sharp-beaked ground finch lives only on Genovesa Island. It eats insects, seeds, and flowers.

Beak shapes and food types

Darwin's finches evolved different beak shapes to tackle different kinds of foods.

Insects

A narrow, pointed beak works like a pair of tweezers to grab and grip small, fast-moving insects.

Mixed diet

A sturdy, curved beak can handle soft foods, but it's also strong enough to crush small seeds.

Seeds

A beak with a heavy upper part that overlaps the lower part and can crack and crush large seeds.

Galápagos penguins

Small but mighty

The Galápagos penguin is the second-smallest species of penguins, standing at around 20 in (50 cm) tall. Unlike other penguin species, which gather in vast flocks, these penguins hang out on the rocky shore in little gangs.

The Galápagos Islands never fail to amaze—so it will come as no surprise that penguins live here. These flightless waterbirds are usually found in the frozen Antarctic and icy Southern Ocean. However, the islands have their own little species—the Galápagos penguin—that's made its way to a warmer part of the world.

The Galápagos straddles the equator, which makes the islands' penguins the only penguin species to live in the northern hemisphere. In other ways, the penguins are just like their southern cousins. Their stiff flipper-like wings are useless for flying—but perfect for powering through the water in pursuit of a fish to eat.

The upper beak is black, but the base of the lower beak is an orange-yellow color, with the occasional bit of pink.

On hot land

For a bird that's built to spend long hours swimming in cold water, the Galápagos penguin can get hot and bothered on the dry, rocky shore. However, the birds can retreat underground to cool lava tubes and other nooks, where they nest and raise their young.

In cold water

With their sleek torpedo-shaped bodies, these penguins are most at home in water. Their glossy, waterproof feathers trap air bubbles that keep the birds warm and also help them float in water, like a life jacket. Nevertheless, Galápagos penguins rarely stray far from land—unlike other penguin species, which may spend months at sea. These tropical birds find all the tasty fish they need within a few hundred feet of the shore and return to land to rest each night.

This species has black feathers on its back and white plumage on its chest.

See where they live

The penguins are found mostly on the western side of the islands, where the water is much colder.

Darwin
Wolf
Pinta
Isabela
Marchena
Genovesa
Santiago
Santa Cruz
Fernandina
Floreana
San Cristóbal
Española

Under threat

The numbers of Galápagos penguins go up and down regularly due to changes in the supply of food. During El Niño times, there's less food around, so many penguins starve. The birds recover in numbers, but slowly. They lay two eggs each year, but usually only one chick survives. In addition, there's a shortage of suitable nesting sites. Conservationists now make shelters constructed from lava, which is helping to boost the numbers of penguins.

Waved albatross

One of the largest birds to visit the Galápagos, the waved albatross spends much of the year far out to sea, soaring effortlessly on its wide wings for weeks on end. It feeds on fish and squid, swooping down to the water's surface to snatch them in its long, snappy beak.

Swallow-tailed gull

When other gulls are heading back to land as night falls, this unusual bird is getting ready to set off on a hunting trip. This Galápagos seabird is the only gull to feed at night. It preys on shoals of squid and fish that rise to the sea's surface in search of food when it gets dark.

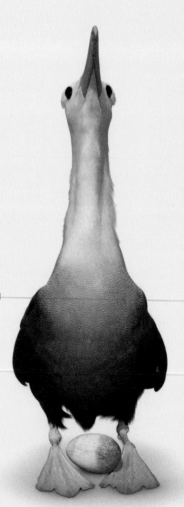

Seabirds

An adult bird weighs only around 6.5 lb (3 kg) but has a wingspan of 8 ft (2.5 m).

With nothing but ocean for hundreds of miles in every direction, the Galápagos Islands are a much needed stopping point for seabirds looking for a place to rest after many days—or even weeks—out at sea.

These seabirds may be just passing through, on their way to somewhere else. Others, such as the waved albatross, come to the islands to breed. There are also seabirds that live all year round on the islands. Some of these, such as the swallow-tailed gull and Galápagos petrel, are found nowhere else. Conservationists are working to protect the sites where seabirds breed on the islands, ensuring that these rare birds will be flying around the Galápagos for many years to come.

Breeding colony

Each March, thousands of waved albatross arrive on Española Island, in the south of the Galápagos. Española and Isla de la Plata—an island much closer to Ecuador—are the only two places on Earth where these big birds breed. Each breeding pair lays just a single egg each year.

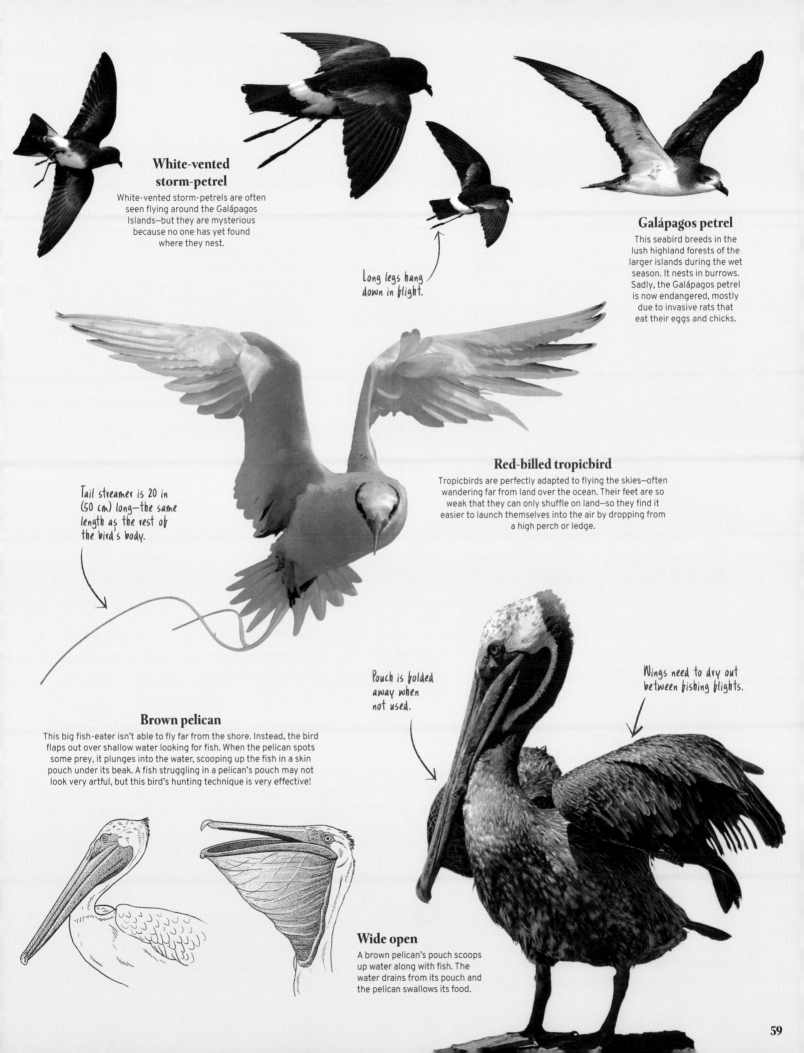

White-vented storm-petrel

White-vented storm-petrels are often seen flying around the Galápagos Islands—but they are mysterious because no one has yet found where they nest.

Long legs hang down in flight.

Galápagos petrel

This seabird breeds in the lush highland forests of the larger islands during the wet season. It nests in burrows. Sadly, the Galápagos petrel is now endangered, mostly due to invasive rats that eat their eggs and chicks.

Red-billed tropicbird

Tropicbirds are perfectly adapted to flying the skies—often wandering far from land over the ocean. Their feet are so weak that they can only shuffle on land—so they find it easier to launch themselves into the air by dropping from a high perch or ledge.

Tail streamer is 20 in (50 cm) long—the same length as the rest of the bird's body.

Brown pelican

This big fish-eater isn't able to fly far from the shore. Instead, the bird flaps out over shallow water looking for fish. When the pelican spots some prey, it plunges into the water, scooping up the fish in a skin pouch under its beak. A fish struggling in a pelican's pouch may not look very artful, but this bird's hunting technique is very effective!

Pouch is folded away when not used.

Wings need to dry out between fishing flights.

Wide open

A brown pelican's pouch scoops up water along with fish. The water drains from its pouch and the pelican swallows its food.

Rocky terrain

Much of the coastline of the Galápagos Islands is covered in dark gray rock made from the molten lava that gushed from volcanoes many years ago.

A couple of Galápagos birds have managed to find a way to live and nest in this habitat. The lava heron's drab feathers help to camouflage it against the gray-black lava rocks.

Shoreline crab hunter

The lava heron is found only in the Galápagos. Unlike most other herons—which hunt in water—the lava heron also finds food on the shore. It stalks intertidal crabs that scuttle across the dark rocks.

← Long but sturdy beak for grabbing prey.

Blue-gray wing feathers have flashes of green and purple. →

Lava heron

This little wading bird lives on the dark rocks around lagoons and in mangrove forests. It watches the water for fish and other creatures before diving in to grab them. The heron mostly has drab blue-gray feathers to match its lava home. It builds its nest in quiet spots among waterside thickets. During the breeding season a male lava heron develops bright orange legs to show off to a female lava heron.

Bare lava rock ↓

Solitary nesters

Lava gulls mostly build their nests on sandy beaches or in dry grass. They are solitary nesters and usually make their nests 328 ft (100 m) apart from each other. Lava gull eggs are dark and speckled, and blend in well with the surroundings.

Red eye with white eyebrows

Black beak

Plumage includes several shades of gray.

Gray feathers blend in with dark rocks.

Lava gull

There are only around eight hundred lava gulls in the world, and they all live in the Galápagos. That makes this seabird the rarest gull species on Earth. The gulls don't fly far out to sea to feed. They usually get what they need by scavenging for pieces of food on the lava field, or snatching baby lizards from the rocks, or grabbing fish from rock pools. They also steal food!

Thief!

Sometimes lava gulls don't need to find their own food because they just steal it from other seabirds returning home from foraging trips. The gulls may even grab it from them in midair! They also raid other birds' nests for eggs and chicks.

Galápagos hawks

Unique to the islands, this handsome hawk is the largest bird of prey living in the Galápagos. It's the top predator on most of the islands—no other land animal is safe from its attacks!

This clever hawk adapts its hunting strategy depending on its target prey. For instance, in the middle of the year, hawks gather above the huge crater of La Cumbre—Fernandina's volcano. They are on the lookout for tasty iguana hatchlings to snap up as they dig themselves out of their nests in the sand. Despite its hunting skills, the Galápagos hawk is vulnerable, with only around three hundred of these large birds of prey left in the wild.

Hawkeyed

Like other hawks in the world, the Galápagos hawk mostly searches for prey while flying slowly high above the ground. When it sees a likely target, the bird dives in for the kill, stomping on its victim and finishing it off with a bite from its hooked beak.

Bird food

The Galápagos hawk is not a picky eater. It preys on a wide range of animals such as locusts, giant centipedes, baby giant tortoises, Galápagos racer snakes, and Galápagos rice rats.

Galápagos giant centipede

A monstrous 12 in (30 cm) long, this centipede has a powerful venom—but it's no match for a hawk in a surprise attack.

Large painted locust

This big, colorful grasshopper becomes more abundant after heavy rains.

Adults have a wingspan of around 4 ft (1.2 m).

Wide fringe of wing feathers allows for slow, controlled flight.

See where it lives

The Galápagos hawk is found across the islands but is now extinct on a few, including San Cristóbal.

Darwin
Wolf
Pinta
Isabela
Marchena
Genovesa
Santiago
Santa Cruz
Fernandina
Floreana
San Cristóbal
Española

Air attack

While the hawk mostly targets prey on the ground, it can also pluck flying birds out of the air. One of the main victims of midair hawk attacks is the Galápagos dove. Found only on the islands, this bird is a small relative of the pigeons seen in cities across the world.

Owl rival

The hawk has been driven out of San Cristóbal and Floreana by humans. Its job on these islands as the top predator has been taken over by the short-eared owl. This bird is usually a night hunter, but it now also searches for food during the day since no hawk rivals are around.

Galápagos racer snake

To stop a snake from fighting back with a venomous bite, the hawk bites off the snake's head.

Baby giant tortoise

The hawk will snatch baby tortoises that have just hatched out of their eggs.

Galápagos rice rat

The hawk preys on this native mammal, as well as the rodent species introduced to the islands by humans.

Boobies

The Galápagos Islands are famous for these large diving seabirds, with brightly colored feet and sharp beaks. Related to gannets, their comical name comes from the Spanish word "bobo," which means clown or stupid.

The birds might have earned this name from their clumsy landings. They are very good fliers but not so agile on the ground. Another reason is that the birds are very tame and not afraid of humans. They sometimes land on the decks of ships far from land. In the days of sailing ships, the hungry crew caught the birds for food. The sailors thought the birds were too stupid to keep away from danger.

Air bag protection

Boobies have squishy sacs of air inside their cheeks, giving them wide heads. These sacs help cushion the impact with the water when the birds plunge headfirst into the sea when hunting.

Dive bombing

Boobies hunt for fish in deep water. They look for prey high above the sea's surface, and then plummet headfirst into the water when they spot some. If they don't hit their target first time, they'll chase it through the water.

The big webbed feet are used for swimming underwater.

Mating dance

Blue-footed boobies will mate any time of the year, usually when it looks like there'll be a good supply of food around for the chicks. Breeding starts with an elaborate courtship dance—another clownish behavior that earns these birds their name.

Stepping on the spot
The courtship dance starts with the male stepping on the spot, lifting up one webbed foot and then the other repeatedly. This shows the female that he's nice and healthy.

Bows head
The male then bows his head, curving his long, flexible neck so his long, pointed beak is pressed onto his chest.

The male's eyes have smaller pupils than the female's eyes.

Three species

There are three kinds of boobies found in the Galápagos Islands. The most common is the blue-footed booby, which nests in many places along the rocky lava shoreline. Around a third of all the world's blue-footed boobies live here. The other two species, the red-footed booby and Nazca booby, are less commonly seen but also nest on some of the islands.

Other boobies

Red-footed booby

The smallest booby species feeds far from land in fish-rich waters above underwater seamounts. The red-footed booby makes its nest in a tree.

Nazca booby

This is the largest booby species. It has an orange beak and gray feet. Like its red-footed cousin, it also hunts far from land.

Adults of both sexes have blue feet.

Feet

The blue color in the birds' feet comes from chemicals in the sardines that they eat. A healthy bird has very bright blue feet.

Offers a gift
Next, the male picks up a stick or a stone and offers it to his mate. She takes it in her mouth and then drops it on the ground.

Sky-pointing
The male now performs a dance move called sky-pointing. He points his beak straight up at the sky, while extending his wings and shrieking.

Female joins in
The female booby joins in the dance. After mating, she lays two or three eggs. The pair use their feet to keep the eggs warm before they hatch.

Losing flight

The flightless cormorant's ancestors could fly—like all the other species of cormorants—and they arrived in the Galápagos by air. Once here, the birds used their wings less and less. They had no need to fly away from danger on these predator-free islands. The birds with the smallest wings found it easier to hunt for food underwater, so the species gradually evolved weaker wings until the birds couldn't fly at all.

Bright blue eye

Long, flexible neck

Strong beak for holding food.

Wing feathers are too short for flight.

Flightless cormorants

Large, strong body for swimming

This large fish-eating bird adds yet another reason to marvel at the uniqueness of the Galápagos Islands.

As its name suggests, this bird cannot fly. It has no need to take to the air because there are no natural predators on the islands for it to escape from. It also doesn't need to fly to feed—instead, it dives deep underwater for its food, mostly fish and octopuses. As a result, evolution has made its wings small and useless.

Webbed feet

Drying out

Despite being a waterbird, the cormorant's feathers are not very waterproof. After a hunt, the bird climbs out of the sea with a series of hops and jumps and spreads its tiny wings to dry them out in the sunshine.

The Galápagos cormorant is the heaviest cormorant in the world.

Nesting

A breeding pair of cormorants dances together, twisting their necks around one another's. They then build a nest on the shore from seaweed.

The female usually lays a clutch of three eggs, and the pair take turns keeping them warm. The eggs take around thirty-five days to hatch.

In the water

Most birds have large chest muscles for powering their wings. However, the flightless cormorant's big muscles are lower down in the legs, which drive it through the water on deep dives. This cormorant is so bottom-heavy that when it swims on the surface, only its long snake-like neck and head poke out of the water.

After a couple of months—if there's still plenty of food in the sea—the female leaves the male to finish off raising the surviving chicks. She then sets off to find another mate to breed with.

Feet

The cormorant has four toes with a thick web of skin between them. Underwater, this webbing turns the foot into a paddle.

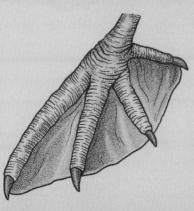

Bird Island

Genovesa is a small island in the northeast of the Galápagos Archipelago. This island is known for the vast amount of birds found there and has therefore earned the nickname "Bird Island."

The horseshoe-shaped island has a large bay, rugged cliffs, and long beaches. Inland, there are lava fields, highlands, and a small crater lake. The variety of habitats on the island supports a rich diversity of seabirds, wading birds, and land birds. Some bird species are year-round residents, while others come to the island just to breed.

Red-billed tropicbird

Waved albatross

Galápagos short-eared owl

Nazca booby

White-bellied storm-petrel

Wedge-rumped storm-petrel

Great frigatebird

Lake Arcturus

Darwin Beach

Darwin Bay

Prince Philip's Steps

Prince Philip's Steps

These steep, rocky steps up onto the eastern headland of Darwin Bay pass through the heart of a seabird colony. All kinds of seabirds are found here, including tropicbirds, storm-petrels, and frigatebirds.

Lake Arcturus

This saltwater crater lake—around 1,640 ft (500 m) across and 100 ft (30 m) deep—lies at the top of Genovesa. Marine iguanas sometimes climb up from the seashore to feed in the lake. Rare species of Darwin's finches live in the surrounding shrubland. This highland habitat is also home to the Galápagos rail, a ground-living bird that feeds on seeds and insects.

See where the island is

Bird Island's official name is Genovesa. It's one of the far, outlying islands in the Galápagos Archipelago.

Darwin
Wolf

Pinta

Marchena

Genovesa

Isabela

Santiago

Santa Cruz

Fernandina

Floreana

San Cristóbal

Española

Franklin's gull

Galápagos fur seal

Semipalmated plover

Wilson's plover

Galápagos dove

Galápagos brown pelican

Yellow-crowned night-heron

Galápagos penguin

Brown noddy tern

Lava heron

Least sandpiper

Black-winged stilt

Red-footed booby

Yellow warbler

Darwin Bay

The island's large bay is named after Charles Darwin—even though he never set foot on Genovesa. This sheltered cove is a haven for sea life, such as sharks and turtles. The sandy coral beach at the top of the bay is known as Darwin Beach, and it's a favorite resting spot for seals and sea lions. The shoreline is a great place to see wading birds and gulls. Tourists visit the beach most days, but no one stays for more than a few hours. No humans are allowed to live on Bird Island.

Protecting songbirds

A male San Cristóbal vermilion flycatcher

More than twenty bird species living in the Galápagos are in serious danger of extinction, including nearly all the species that are found only on the islands.

Many of the small songbirds that live in the different land habitats of the islands are endangered. These species include some of the Galápagos mockingbirds and many of the Darwin's finches. Each bird species faces a unique set of threats, so conservationists have to come up with a survival plan tailored to each type of bird. These plans involve fighting back against invasive, or non-native, species and working with local people to protect habitats.

Extinct songbird

The San Cristóbal vermilion flycatcher, a tiny songbird just 4 in (10 cm) long, was declared extinct in 2016. Habitat loss probably played a large part in this brightly colored insect-eater's extinction. As its home range was cleared for farmland and buildings, the bird's food—insects—began to disappear, and the species didn't have enough food to survive.

Coming home

There have been no Floreana mockingbirds living on Floreana Island since 1888. They were killed off by the rats and cats introduced by settlers. Plans are now being drawn up to reintroduce the birds to Floreana, using birds bred from the Floreana mockingbirds that still live on Champion and Gardner, two islets close to Floreana.

Incomer

The smooth-billed ani was brought to the Galápagos Islands in 1970 by farmers who hoped it would eat the ticks that troubled their cattle. The bird doesn't eat ticks but feasts instead on insects. The ani has thrived on the islands but at a cost to native birds, who have to compete with it for food.

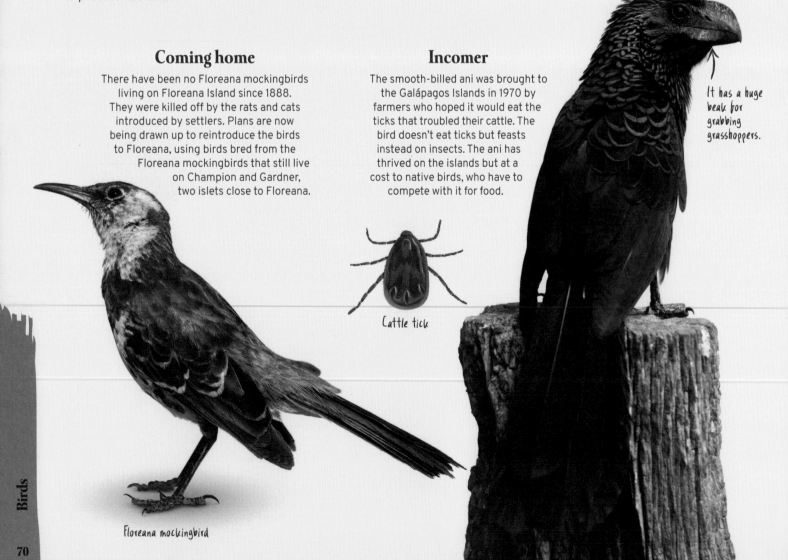

It has a huge beak for grabbing grasshoppers.

Cattle tick

Floreana mockingbird

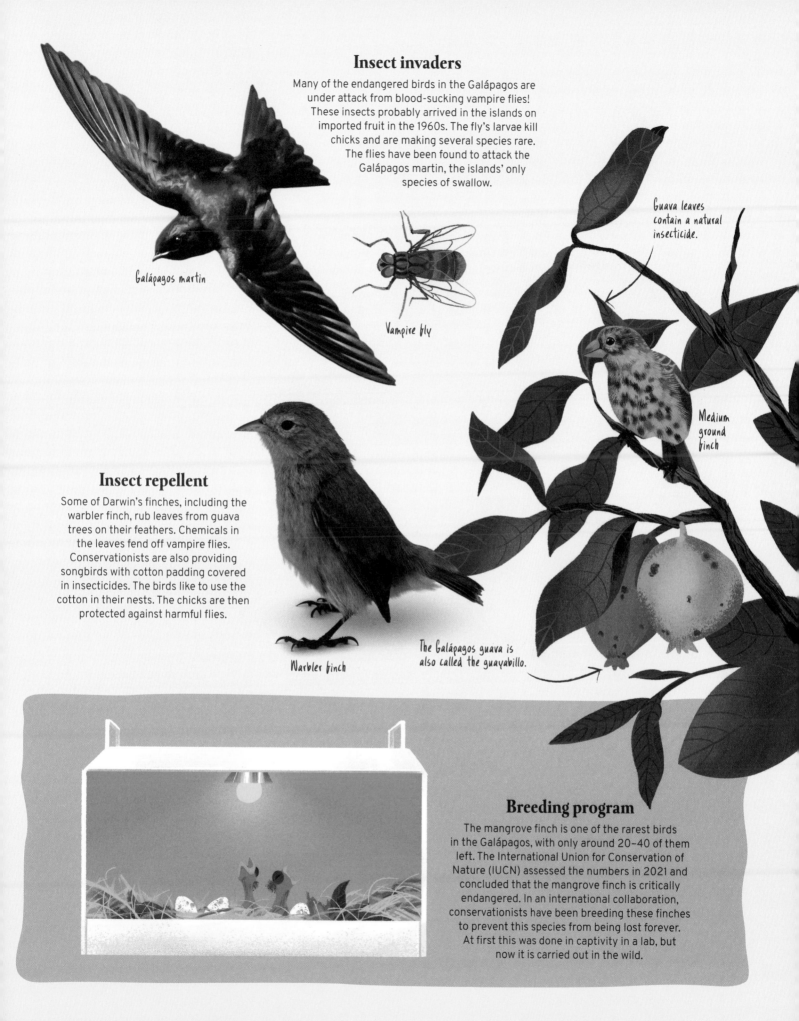

Insect invaders

Many of the endangered birds in the Galápagos are under attack from blood-sucking vampire flies! These insects probably arrived in the islands on imported fruit in the 1960s. The fly's larvae kill chicks and are making several species rare. The flies have been found to attack the Galápagos martin, the islands' only species of swallow.

Galápagos martin

Vampire fly

Guava leaves contain a natural insecticide.

Medium ground finch

Insect repellent

Some of Darwin's finches, including the warbler finch, rub leaves from guava trees on their feathers. Chemicals in the leaves fend off vampire flies. Conservationists are also providing songbirds with cotton padding covered in insecticides. The birds like to use the cotton in their nests. The chicks are then protected against harmful flies.

Warbler finch

The Galápagos guava is also called the guayabillo.

Breeding program

The mangrove finch is one of the rarest birds in the Galápagos, with only around 20–40 of them left. The International Union for Conservation of Nature (IUCN) assessed the numbers in 2021 and concluded that the mangrove finch is critically endangered. In an international collaboration, conservationists have been breeding these finches to prevent this species from being lost forever. At first this was done in captivity in a lab, but now it is carried out in the wild.

The waters around Darwin and Wolf Islands, in the northwest of the archipelago, contain more sharks than any other place on Earth.

Marine life

The oceans around the Galápagos Islands are teeming with wildlife. Although the islands are home to some amazingly unusual land animals, there are many, many more marine, or seafaring, animals living in the cold waters surrounding the islands. These creatures include vast shoals of fish, fierce sharks, and the world's largest animals—whales. The volcanic nature of the islands can also be seen on the seabed in the region. Plumes of superheated, mineral-rich water surges out of vents, creating a thriving habitat for life in the murky depths.

Galápagos sharks, silky sharks, and black-tip sharks hunting fish.

Giant tube worms

These tube worms live around hydrothermal vents on the ocean floor. The worms get all their nutrients from bacteria that live inside them. The bacteria are able to turn chemicals in the water into food.

Galápagos shark

Many types of sharks are found in the waters around the Galápagos Islands, including the Galápagos shark, which hunts fish and octopuses.

Marine life

Pointed pectoral fins are used for swimming.

So far, almost three thousand species of animals have been found in the waters around the Galápagos Islands. This diverse range of marine life includes the blue whale—the largest animal that has ever lived—and a lime-green sea urchin the size of a Ping-Pong ball.

The waters around the Galápagos are full of life as the animals feed on the nutrients that the currents bring from the ocean's depths. Most of the time, there is plenty of food to go around in the cold, clear waters. Much deeper down, however, there is a completely different community of life, centered around jets of super-hot, chemical-rich water that shoots out of the seabed. Even down there, the Galápagos Islands are incredibly special.

Giant manta ray

This enormous ray swims by flapping its wing-like fins up and down as if flying though the water. Weighing up to 3.3 tons (3 tonnes), this monster fish is harmless to humans.

Red-lipped batfish

This pouty-faced fish is widespread in the coastal waters of the Galápagos. It patrols patches of sandy seabed by "walking" on its leg-like fins.

Galápagos sea lion

Most at home hunting for fish, this small species of sea lion is found only in the Galápagos. After feeding, the sea lions come onto land to rest, taking naps on quiet beaches or even busy streets.

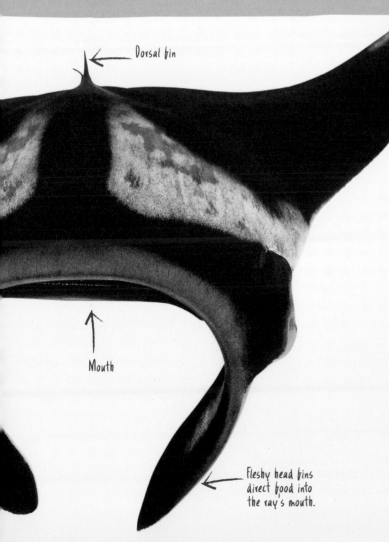

Dorsal fin

Mouth

Fleshy head fins direct food into the ray's mouth.

Ocean seaweeds

The seaweeds along the coast of the islands are adapted to life in different underwater habitats. Kelp grows in rough waters where waves crash into the shore. It floats upright in deep water, so its fronds can catch as much light as possible—which it needs to make its own food—in the moving water. By contrast, sea lettuce is much smaller and spreads across the seafloor in calmer, clear waters with plenty of sunlight. Sea lettuce grows closer to the surface—on intertidal rocks and in rock pools.

Frond

Bulb

Holdfast

Stipe (trunk)

Kelp can form underwater forests and provide shelter for marine life.

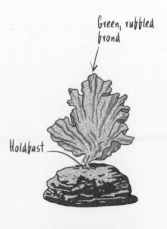

Green, ruffled frond

Holdfast

Sea lettuce is eaten by many different sea animals.

Sea lions
and fur seals

The many sandy coves and quiet beaches around the shores of the Galápagos Islands are often filled with herds of sleepy sea lions.

They have to shuffle out of the water to rest after hunting trips out at sea for fish. With large males reaching 8 ft (2.5 m) in length and weighing up to 550 lb (250 kg), Galápagos sea lions are by far the largest animals on the islands. They are joined here by Galápagos fur seals, which are around half the size of the sea lions.

Galápagos fur seal

A close relative of the sea lion, this smaller Galápagos species has longer fur and bigger ears. It hunts at night and catches fish and squid near the surface of the water.

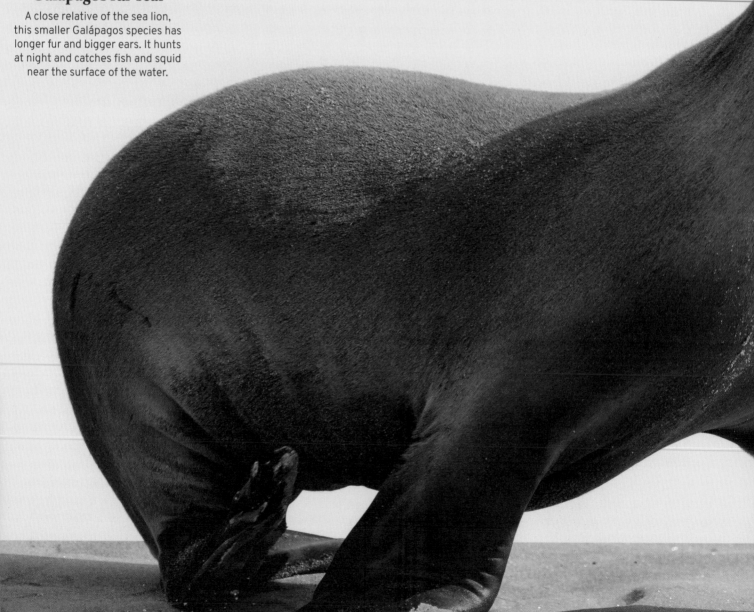

Galápagos sea lion

This species spends days at sea following shoals of sardines. On land, the sea lion walks on its four flipper-like feet. This is different from how true, or earless, seals move on land—they have much shorter flippers and move around by wiggling!

Tiny external ear

Large eye

Sensitive nose

Long whiskers

Feeding

Sea lions are very agile in water. They see better underwater than in air, and their sensitive whiskers can pick up currents created by nearby fish. This allows the sea lions to find and catch food in the dark.

Threats

Sea lions need to keep an eye out for hungry sharks and orca whales. Their biggest threat, however, is El Niño. During this natural change in the climate—which happens every few years—the ocean warms up. This causes the number of fish to drop fast in the ocean around the Galápagos. With little or no food, many of the sea lions—especially young ones—starve.

Big flippers

Sea lions search for food close to the shore to avoid being eaten by sharks or killer whales.

Beachmasters

During the breeding season, the biggest male sea lions spend all their time on the beach, each defending patches of sand. Known as "beachmasters," these males attack other males entering their territory, and they mate with the females that come to raise their young on that section of beach.

Sperm whale
The largest toothed animal on Earth, this whale is seen near to the islands all year round. It dives deep to catch giant squid.

Common dolphin
These midsize dolphins sometimes travel in huge pods, or groups, containing hundreds of individuals. They often gather and hunt above seamounts—undersea hills hidden beneath the waves.

Blue whale
Weighing 165 tons (150 tonnes), the blue whale is both the largest whale and animal in the world. This titan of the sea is a regular visitor to the islands, where it feasts on mouthfuls of krill and other small crustaceans.

Bottlenose dolphin
This large dolphin is the cetacean most easily spotted from the islands since it frequently comes close to the shore. It also likes to swim in the wake of boats and ships.

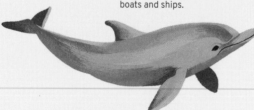

Striped dolphin
Darker than the other Galápagos dolphins, the striped dolphin spends most of its time far out to sea. It has a pattern of black and gray stripes on its back and sides, and a cream or pink underside.

Whales and dolphins

Whales and dolphins belong to a group of sea mammals called cetaceans. Twenty-four different species of cetaceans live in or visit the waters around the Galápagos Islands.

A few of the species, including the orca and common dolphin, spend the whole year—perhaps their whole lives—around the islands. Most of the whales and dolphins, however, are just visiting for a short time, passing through the wide channels between the islands on their way elsewhere. One such visitor is the largest whale of all—the blue whale.

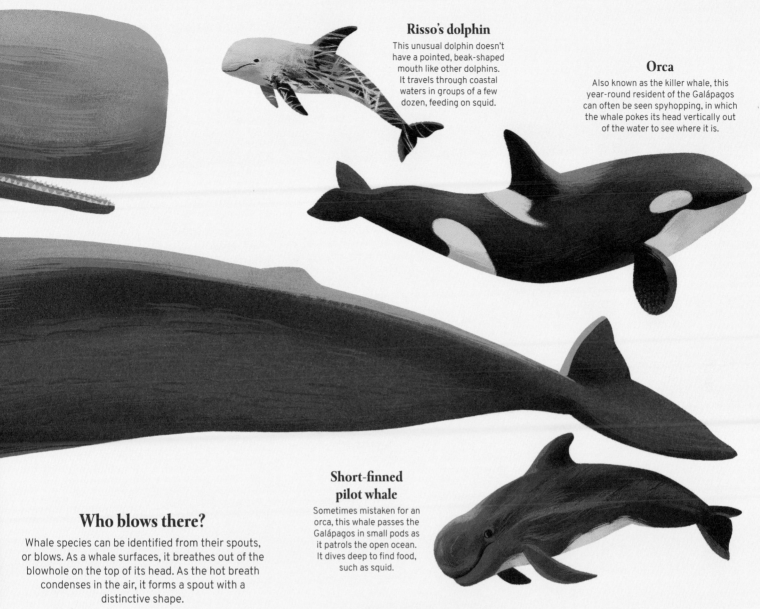

Risso's dolphin

This unusual dolphin doesn't have a pointed, beak-shaped mouth like other dolphins. It travels through coastal waters in groups of a few dozen, feeding on squid.

Orca

Also known as the killer whale, this year-round resident of the Galápagos can often be seen spyhopping, in which the whale pokes its head vertically out of the water to see where it is.

Short-finned pilot whale

Sometimes mistaken for an orca, this whale passes the Galápagos in small pods as it patrols the open ocean. It dives deep to find food, such as squid.

Blainville's beaked whale

An occasional visitor to the islands, this whale looks like a giant dolphin, but it's not closely related.

Who blows there?

Whale species can be identified from their spouts, or blows. As a whale surfaces, it breathes out of the blowhole on the top of its head. As the hot breath condenses in the air, it forms a spout with a distinctive shape.

Blue whale spout

This giant produces a balloon-shaped column up to 20 ft (6 m) high and visible from a long distance.

Sperm whale spout

The spout produced by this whale is slanted and is around 10 ft (3 m) high.

Orca spout

This whale has a bushy, rounded spout that stays close to the water's surface.

Echolocation

Dolphins and other toothed whales use a sonar system, known as echolocation, to hunt and navigate. They give out high-pitched clicks, which echo off the seabed and other animals in the area. The echoes are received by the dolphins' lower jaw—rather than their ears. They use the information from the echoes to build up a picture of what is around them in the water.

Beach nests

Like all reptiles, sea turtles breath air. They must lay their eggs out of water, so the babies growing inside don't drown. Female turtles pull themselves out of the sea onto beaches and lay eggs in nests—deep holes in the sand. When they hatch, the baby turtles race down the beach into the sea. Male turtles stay at sea their whole lives. Females, however, return as adults to the beach where they hatched. They lay their eggs there and the cycle continues.

The upper part of the shell is called the carapace.

The beak-shaped mouth is used for slicing food.

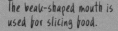

Sea turtles

The sparkling, clear waters around the Galápagos are visited by different kinds of turtles. The most common is the green sea turtle, and the islands have their very own subspecies— the Galápagos green sea turtle—which breeds only here.

It spends much of its time in shallow water, such as the lagoons along the islands' coasts. It's called "green" because that's the color of its fat, beneath the shell. Sea turtles were once widely eaten by people but are now protected in many areas. Turtles are distant relatives of the giant tortoises that live on land, but they have adapted superbly to a life in water. The upper and lower part of their shell forms a sleek diving suit, and their front limbs are shaped like flippers for propelling them through water.

The upper part of the shell is called the carapace.

Green sea turtles can grow to 5 ft (1.5 m) long.

The shell is yellow on the lower part, called the plastron.

Occasional visitors

There are seven species of sea turtles in the world. Apart from the resident green sea turtles, three other species are occasional visitors to the Galápagos Islands. As far as we know, none of the visitors breed there.

Hawksbill sea turtle

A little smaller than the green sea turtle, this sea turtle feeds mostly on sponges. It's now very rare, mostly due to people killing it for its beautiful shell.

Leatherback sea turtle

This is the largest sea turtle, even bigger than the giant tortoise. It's 6.5 ft (2 m) long and even longer with its front flippers outstretched. Leatherbacks are very good jellyfish hunters.

Mixed diet

The Galápagos green sea turtle changes its diet as it grows. Young turtles are mostly carnivorous, and prey on crabs, jellyfish, and other small marine animals. By the time the turtles have become adults, they have switched to being herbivorous, grazing mostly on seagrass and seaweed.

Olive ridley sea turtle

Around half the size of the green sea turtle, this olive-colored turtle feeds mostly on fish, shellfish, and other small animals.

Sally Lightfoot crab

This brightly colored crabs are a common sight scuttling around the rugged shoreline of the Galápagos Islands. Growing to 8 in (20 cm) across, this big crab is very successful because it will eat almost anything.

Like other crabs, the Sally Lightfoot breathes using gills. Crabs' gills are special because they can operate in air—as long as they are kept moist—as well as in water. This allows the eye-catching crabs to spend a lot of time high up on the shore, searching for food.

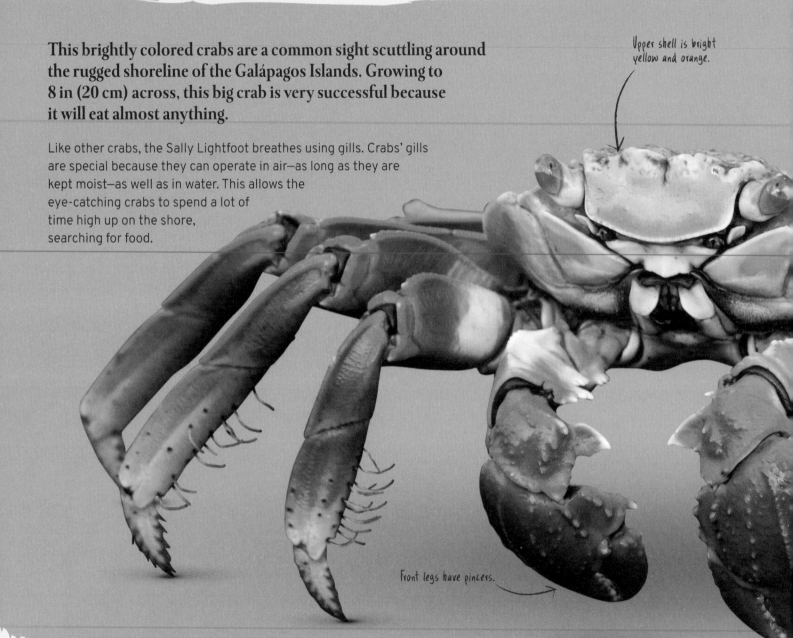

Upper shell is bright yellow and orange.

Front legs have pincers.

Getting brighter

This nimble-footed crab is very hard to catch, and so it doesn't try to stay out of sight—and the adults' red, yellow, and blue markings make them highly visible. However, a young Sally Lightfoot crab needs to be more careful. After hatching from its egg, the tiny crab larvae swim in the water and eat plankton. When it has grown enough to sink to the bottom, the baby crabs crawl onto land. It's dark with red spots and that helps it to blend into the rocks. To grow larger, a crab has to shed its hard outer shell. Each time a young Sally Lightfoot molts, the new shell underneath is a little more colorful.

Walking on water?

How the Sally Lightfoot crab got its name is a little bit of a mystery. The best explanation is that when the crab scuttles around in the shallows, it looks like it's walking on water. It is "lightfooted" and nimble in its movements.

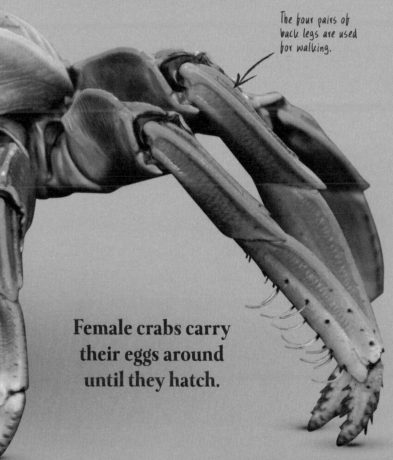

The four pairs of back legs are used for walking.

Female crabs carry their eggs around until they hatch.

Cannibal crab

Sally Lightfoot crabs eat anything, from ticks plucked from the skin of a marine iguana to the afterbirth of a sea lion. They also eat each other if there is nothing else available. The baby crabs' camouflage helps protect them from the older crabs!

Super powers

Sally Lightfoot crabs are equipped with a surprising set of skills, making them very successful at surviving in the Galápagos.

Running Fast on its eight feet, the Sally Lightfoot crab can run just as quickly backward and sideways as it can forward.

Climbing There are claws on the ends of the crab's walking legs. The crab uses them to climb up and over rocks along the shore. It can even walk straight up a vertical wall.

Jumping Gaps between rocks are no barrier to a Sally Lightfoot crab. It just leaps across them and then scuttles on its way!

Silky shark

This smooth-skinned shark is an ocean wanderer that lives in tropical waters across the world. The shark visits the Galápagos to feed on fish, squid, and crabs.

Sharks

Close to the coasts of the Galápagos Islands—and occasionally visible in the gloomy water—sharks are always circling. They are attracted by the fish and other sea life that crowd into the fertile waters fed by ocean currents that bring a rich flow of nutrients.

Sharks have been around for more than 450 million years and are perfectly adapted to hunting in the ocean. Different species target different foods—from the billions of plankton floating in the cloudy water to crunchy sea urchins on the seabed.

The dorsal fin is tall and pointed.

Galápagos shark

Despite the name, this 10 ft (3 m) long species lives across the world. It can always be found hunting in the waters around islands—often very remote ones like the Galápagos.

Whitetip reef shark

This medium-sized shark rarely strays far from the rocky coastline. It sleeps during the day in underwater caves, coming out at night to hunt for fish and octopuses.

Galápagos bullhead shark

Only 3.3 ft (1 m) long, this shark has a wide, flat mouth and large nostrils. At night, it forages on the seabed for shellfish.

Grey reef shark

The grey reef shark swims slowly most of the time, but it can achieve speeds of 25 mph (40 kph) when chasing prey.

Whale shark

The largest fish of all, this giant grows to nearly 62 ft (19 m) long and has thousands of teeth—but they are only tiny. Despite their size, whale sharks do not hunt. Instead they eat plankton, which they filter from seawater.

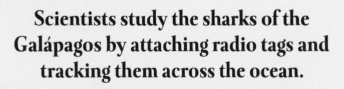

Scientists study the sharks of the Galápagos by attaching radio tags and tracking them across the ocean.

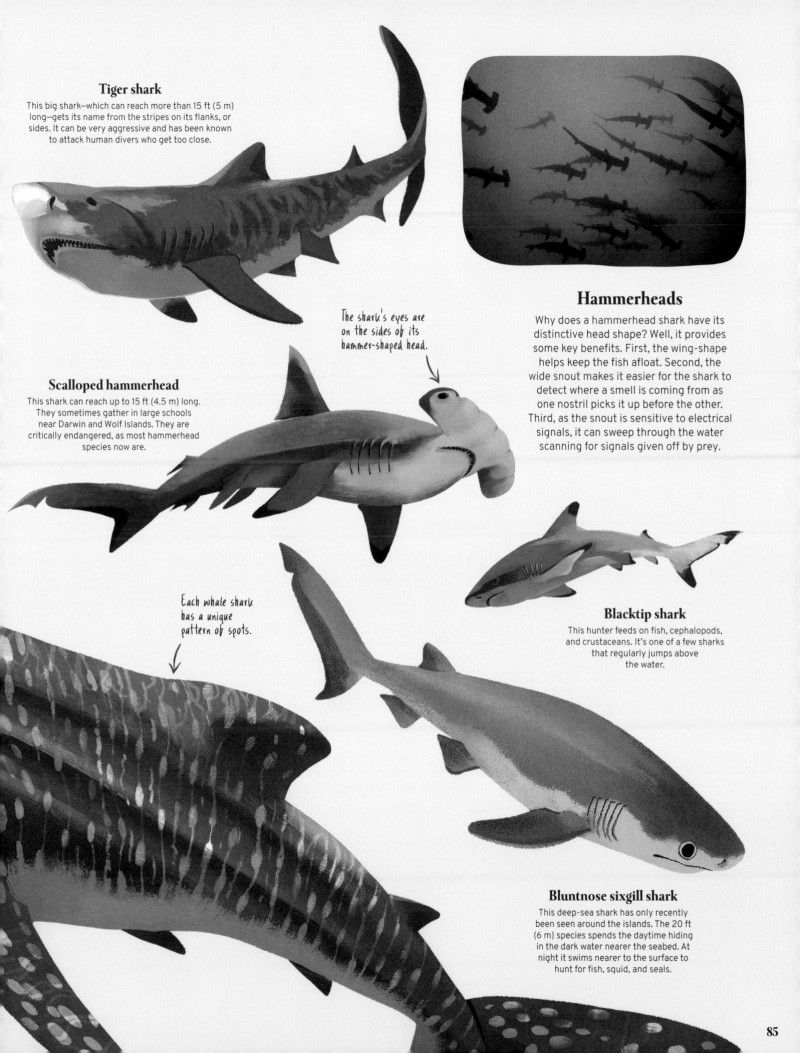

Tiger shark

This big shark—which can reach more than 15 ft (5 m) long—gets its name from the stripes on its flanks, or sides. It can be very aggressive and has been known to attack human divers who get too close.

Hammerheads

Why does a hammerhead shark have its distinctive head shape? Well, it provides some key benefits. First, the wing-shape helps keep the fish afloat. Second, the wide snout makes it easier for the shark to detect where a smell is coming from as one nostril picks it up before the other. Third, as the snout is sensitive to electrical signals, it can sweep through the water scanning for signals given off by prey.

The shark's eyes are on the sides of its hammer-shaped head.

Scalloped hammerhead

This shark can reach up to 15 ft (4.5 m) long. They sometimes gather in large schools near Darwin and Wolf Islands. They are critically endangered, as most hammerhead species now are.

Blacktip shark

This hunter feeds on fish, cephalopods, and crustaceans. It's one of a few sharks that regularly jumps above the water.

Each whale shark has a unique pattern of spots.

Bluntnose sixgill shark

This deep-sea shark has only recently been seen around the islands. The 20 ft (6 m) species spends the daytime hiding in the dark water nearer the seabed. At night it swims nearer to the surface to hunt for fish, squid, and seals.

Deep-sea life

Chemicals in the water form a black cloud that looks like smoke.

In 1979, a deep-sea submersible named Alvin dived 8,530 ft (2,600 m) down to a volcanic region of seabed, north of the Galápagos.

They discovered a jet of water coming out of the seabed that was 716°F (380°C)! This was the first-known hydrothermal vent. Bacteria living around the vent absorb the minerals spewing upward and use their energy to make food—which supports the rest of the food chain. As producers of food, this makes these bacteria equivalent to light-absorbing plants and algae that grow on land and sunlit seas. The entire food chain is independent of sunlight—something unique in the natural world!

Crabs

The mysterious crabs living around the vents have furry pincers. They use the hairs to collect bacteria from the water, which is thought to be their main food. The crabs may also eat other shellfish that live on the seafloor.

Tube worms

Growing up to 10 ft (3 m) long, these are distant relatives of earthworms. To protect themselves they close their tube opening if they are touched or feel any form of threat.

Cold water trickles into the seabed.

Magma heats the water in the rocks.

Black smokers

Hydrothermal vents are like hot springs that gush out of the seafloor. The water is full of chemicals that form dark clouds as they hit the cold water. This is why the vents are nicknamed "black smokers." Cold seawater trickles down through cracks in the seabed. It travels incredibly deep, where it's heated by hot rock, called magma, far below the seafloor. Great pressure from the weight of the ocean and rock above the water stops it from boiling as it shoots up back to the seafloor and out of the vents.

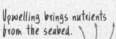

Spiraling gyre above the seamount helps keep the nutrients there.

Upwelling brings nutrients from the seabed.

Surface current

Undercurrent

THIS DIAGRAM IS NOT TO SCALE

Seamounts

The seafloor around the Galápagos Islands isn't flat. It's covered in seamounts, which are old volcanoes now submerged below the ocean's surface. They range from around 328 ft to 9,843 ft (100 m to 3,000 m) in height. The waters above and around seamounts are full of wildlife. Ocean currents bring nutrients from the seabed up the sides of these mounts. This attracts plankton, which in turn attracts fish, seabirds, and other hunters to feed in the waters above the hidden summits.

Shellfish

The first hydrothermal vent found at the Galápagos was nicknamed "Clambake" because it was easily hot enough to cook shellfish. However, heat-loving deep-sea clams thrive in these waters.

Mussels

Some of the world's largest mussels live around the deep-sea vents of the Galápagos. Their shells can grow as long as 16 in (40 cm), which is around the size of a shoebox!

← Deposits of rocky chemicals from the hot water build up around the vents to form tall chimneys.

Alvinella worms

The bristled worms that live around black smokers are named after Alvin, the submersible used to discover the vents.

Galápagos rift shrimp

This pink-colored shrimp probably grazes on the mats of bacteria growing on the rocky seafloor around the vents.

Marine Reserve

The Galápagos Islands are a protected area, a place where wildlife is left to live unaffected by humans as much as possible. In addition to the land, the waters around the islands are protected too, in an area called the Galápagos Marine Reserve.

The reserve was set up in 1978 and is home to almost three thousand species of sharks, turtles, whales, and many other kinds of marine life. It's a great place for scientists to study wild ocean animals. The reserve currently covers 51,352 sq miles (133,000 sq km). It's one of the largest areas of protected ocean in the world. In 2021, Ecuador announced that they will be increasing the conservation area by an additional 23,166 sq miles (60,000 sq km).

Pinta

Genovesa

Isabela

Marchena

Santiago

Fernandina

Santa Cruz

San Cristóbal

Española

Floreana

 Sanctuary area

 Boundary of reserve

Sanctuaries

The Galápagos Marine Reserve has a number of sanctuary areas. These places include important habitats needing special protection and feeding areas for the islands' penguins and sea lions.

Fishing zone

Only Ecuadorian boats are allowed to fish in a large area around the islands, known as an exclusive economic zone. There are hopes that the marine reserve will be extended to fill more of this area.

 Exclusive economic zone

Galápagos Islands

Ecuador

Fishing control

Only small fishing boats based on the Galápagos Islands are allowed to catch fish in the reserve. No big "factory" fishing boats are allowed in. Even local fishing boats are banned from the sanctuary areas.

Coral reef

The Marine Reserve protects the fragile coral reefs around the islands. The main reefs are near Wolf and Darwin Islands. Only a few tourists get to visit these every year. The rules of the reserve state that visitors must not touch the coral or interfere with any wildlife, such as sea slugs.

Starry night sea slug

Protecting the seabed

Trawling is banned in the reserve—this destructive way of fishing uses nets to scrape up fish from the seabed. The ban protects the fragile habitats on the seabed and the creatures living there, such as the batfish.

Mangroves

The dense forests that grow out into the ocean are havens for wildlife, such as herons. These birds feed on the fish that swim among the mangroves' underwater roots.

Sandy beaches

The Galápagos green sea turtles use sandy beaches for making their nests. This is the only place in the world where the turtles lay their eggs, so these beaches need to be carefully protected.

Rocky shores

The distinctive rocky shorelines of the archipelago are made from lava that once plunged into the sea. These shores are home to some of the islands' most iconic species, including the Galápagos penguin, blue-footed booby, and marine iguana.

There are around six hundred plant species found naturally in the Galápagos—and another 825 that have arrived with humans!

Plants

The plant life of the Galápagos has a unique character. There are just six hundred plant species (flowering plants and ferns) native to the islands, compared to at least twenty thousand in the rest of Ecuador. Around one-third of the island plants are found nowhere else on Earth. Plants that are small in other parts of the world have close relatives in the Galápagos that grow to the size of trees. Natural selection has transformed the islands' small set of plants into a fully functioning ecosystem with jungles, dry woodlands, and swampy bogs.

A Scalesia forest in the Galápagos Islands.

Plants

Plants are the foundations of habitats. They sit at the base of food chains—their leaves, seeds, and fruit provide food for many of the islands' insects, reptiles, and birds.

Most of the Galápagos Islands are uninhabited and protected, which allows the islands' unique trees, shrubs, and other plants to continue to thrive. The climate of the Galápagos Islands creates five main habitats, or plant zones. Each zone receives a different amount of rainfall, which supports a particular mixture of plants. Lowland regions, usually near to the ocean, are generally drier than the areas of the islands that are higher up or farther inland.

Darwin's cotton

Growing in dry woodlands away from the coast, this large shrub can reach 10 ft (3 m) high. Its bright yellow flowers are often as big as a human hand. The flowers appear after heavy rain and produce seeds that split open to reveal fluffy strands of cotton. Birds collect the fluff and use it as nesting material.

Mangrove

Fringing the coast, where the seas are calm and shallow, forests of mangrove trees grow out into the water.

Arid zone

The dry lowlands, just inland from the coast, are dominated by cacti and other plants that survive well with little water.

Island plant zones

The five distinct plant zones on the islands are situated at different altitudes (heights). Each zone receives a different amount of rainfall. The northern sides of the islands tend to have larger dry areas than the southern sides.

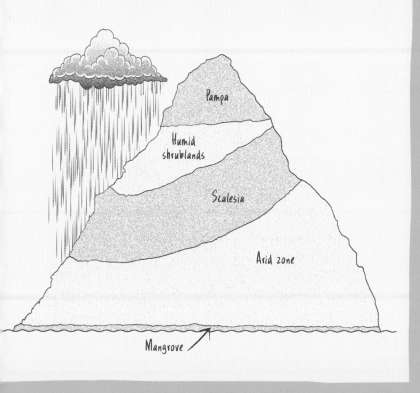

Pampa

The highest areas get so much rain that the soil is swampy and waterlogged. Known as the pampa zone, grasses, mosses, and tree ferns grow well here.

Scalesia

On the slopes of inland hills, forests of Scalesia trees grow. These plants are unique to the Galápagos Islands.

Humid shrublands

Higher up, the Scalesia forest gives way to a damp, dense jungle of low-growing shrubs and ferns.

Darwin
Wolf
Pinta
Isabela
Marchena
Genovesa
Santiago
Fernandina
Santa Cruz
Floreana
San Cristóbal
Española

Mangroves

Many of the beaches and lagoons in the sheltered parts of the Galápagos Islands' coastline are home to mangrove forests—with trees that can grow in seawater.

This habitat is dominated by three species of trees—known as red, black, and white mangrove—all of which take over the shallow seas and grow out over the water. Mangroves are tough—they need to be able to survive in seawater. The mangrove forests of the Galápagos are ancient, having grown here for many thousands of years.

Red mangrove tree

White leaves

Growing out of seawater means that white mangrove trees and black mangrove trees have to be able to cope with a lot of salt. The plants get rid of the unwanted salt at night through holes in their leaves. The trees' leaves are often covered with white crystals of salt.

Floating fruit

The fruit of white and black mangrove trees are able to float. When ripe, they plop into the water and are eventually washed up on shore. The fruit then sprout into mangrove trees. When fully grown, some mangroves reach heights of 66 ft (20 m).

Saltwort and saltbush

Cell

Salty water

Sac with salt

Fleshy leaves

Older leaf falls off.

Water and salt travel upward.

Saltwort is another plant in the Galápagos that can handle very high levels of salt. Salty water travels up through the shrub's roots to its fleshy leaves. Cells inside the leaves remove the salt from the water and store it in sacs. Older leaves eventually contain so much salt that they fall off. Saltbush is also a salt-resistant plant.

Saltbush

Aerial roots

Mangrove trees have woody roots that lift the branches and leaves above the sea's surface. Roots need to take in air, but they can't when they are underwater or buried in the waterlogged seabed. For this reason, mangroves have special roots growing above the water. These aerial roots have holes to let vital air into the root system.

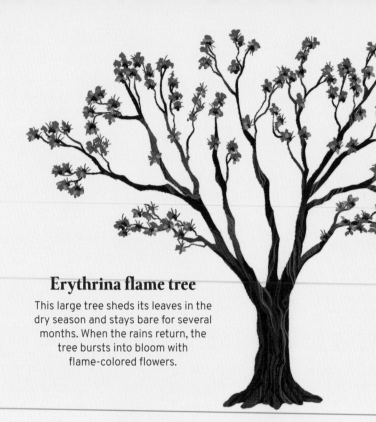

Erythrina flame tree

This large tree sheds its leaves in the dry season and stays bare for several months. When the rains return, the tree bursts into bloom with flame-colored flowers.

Sharp spines stop birds from landing on the cactus.

Plants of the arid zone

On the larger islands of the Galápagos, the land between the coastline and the highlands tends to be very dry, or arid. This is because the clouds usually drop their rain on the hillsides. As a result, lower areas closer to the coastline receive little water.

Arid zones are especially large on the northern sides of the islands. This is because most rain falls on the southern sides of the central highlands. The northern areas are in a "rain shadow." Only plants, such as cacti, that can store water for long periods can survive in arid zones.

Giant prickly pear

This is the most common and the largest cactus on the islands. In some places, it grows up to 40 ft (12 m) tall. The big fleshy pads are the stems. Water is stored inside the spongy interior of the fleshy pads and the tall stem.

Needle-leafed daisy

To save water, this shrub has short, narrow leaves, similar to pine needles. Compared to the larger, flat leaves of other plants, this daisy's leaves have a much smaller surface area, with fewer tiny openings through which water can escape.

Prickly food

The cactus is an important source of food for both land iguanas and giant tortoises. They eat the pads and fruits. Cactus finches feed on the flowers and seeds. On islands where there are no cactus-eating animals, the prickly pears are much less prickly!

Pearlberry

This tall, spindly tree has bright green leaves and white flowers, which produce white oval berries that look like pearls.

Lava cactus

This is the smallest cactus species on the islands, growing to around 24 in (60 cm) tall. As its name suggests, the lava cactus grows out of the lava fields of the arid zone. It forms clumps of spiky stems, spreading out up to 6.5 ft (2 m) across.

Candelabra cactus

Growing to 30 ft (9 m) high on some islands, this cactus gets its name from the way it branches out to the sides, making it look like an old-fashioned candleholder. The cactus is mostly made of a thick spongy stem. The leaves are reduced to the tiny spines that protect it from hungry animals.

Desert thorn

This spiky little shrub fills in the gaps left by larger plants. Narrow leaves grow around the plant's branches, which all end in a sharp spike. After the rains, the desert thorn flowers and produces red berries.

Scalesia

The forests covering the hills of the Galápagos are made up of an unusual tree called Scalesia. There are three types of Scalesia tree.

Despite having tall trunks and sturdy woody branches, Scalesia aren't related to any tree you'll see in a forest in other parts of the world. Instead, they have evolved from small shrubby plants related to daisies, marigolds, and even lettuces! The seeds of the ancestors of Scalesia were probably carried to the Galápagos Islands by birds.

See where they are

This map shows the islands where the main type of Scalesia tree species grows.

Daisy tree

The three Scalesia tree species evolved in a competition for sunlight. No other plants that could survive on the dry, rocky slopes of the Galápagos grew very tall. Whichever plant could evolve to reach for the sky would leave the others in the shade and take over.

Life and death

Scalesia forests grow in a cycle. During wet periods, the forests grow fastest. It takes around fifteen years for the trees to reach 33 ft (10 m) tall. As El Niño approaches, growth slows and Scalesia saplings sprout on the forest floor. Then drought hits the islands and the older, taller trees die. When the next rains arrive, the saplings shoot up to take the dead trees' place.

Wet period

10 ft (3 m)

Dry El Niño

33 ft (10 m)

Wet period

Dead trees

Saplings replace the dead trees.

Plants on plants

The Scalesia forests are full of epiphytes, which are plants that grow on other plants. They use tall plants to reach more sunlight.

Moss is a common epiphyte on Scalesia trees. Mosses have simple bodies. They take water in through their tiny leaves since they don't have roots.

This **Buttonhole orchid** is one of the island's main epiphytes. Their roots cling to tree trunks and take in moisture from the air and bark.

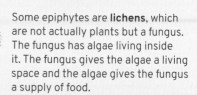

Some epiphytes are **lichens**, which are not actually plants but a fungus. The fungus has algae living inside it. The fungus gives the algae a living space and the algae gives the fungus a supply of food.

Humid shrublands

Miconia zone

Santa Cruz and San Cristóbal, two of the oldest islands, have a particular shrub zone made up mostly of a plant called Miconia. Its flowers can turn the high hillsides pink, and in times of drought the plant's long, green leaves turn dark red.

In the highlands of the larger Galápagos Islands, the air is very humid—it contains a lot of water vapor. The humidity is ideal for many of the islands' plants, and they grow together in a zone called "humid shrublands."

When the air gets too humid, the water in it condenses (changes from a gas to a liquid) and falls as rain. The rain and humidity support a lush shrubland that grows all year round. The tall Scalesia trees that grow lower down the slopes become rarer since they are crowded out by thick growths of shrubs and ferns.

Brown zone

There is another zone in the Galápagos called the "brown zone". It's much smaller than the other zones. It gets its name because it appears to be this color from a distance. This is due to epiphytes, such as mosses and lichens, which cover and hang from the branches of the trees and some shrubs. Epiphytes are also called "air plants" because they get moisture straight from the air. The misty slopes of the Galápagos highlands are an ideal place for them to thrive.

Slow-motion invader

The native plants in Santa Cruz's humid shrublands are being overrun by the quinine tree. The plant was introduced in 1946. It produces seeds much faster than the native plants and grows taller, stealing their light.

Pampa

Covering the tops of the islands' tallest hills is a plant zone called the "pampa." This word comes from the South American language Quechua and means "plain."

The plants growing in the pampa are mostly grasses, sedges, and ferns. This plant zone is the wettest land habitat on the islands, and small plants are better suited to the damp conditions. Few trees and shrubs grow here because their roots can't cope with the shallow, waterlogged soil.

Tree fern

The tallest plants in the pampa are Galápagos tree ferns, which can reach a height of 10 ft (3 m). The ferns often grow out of cracks, sinkholes, and craters on the hilltops.

Lichens

Many of the islands' lichens live in the swampy pampa. Lichens aren't plants—they are fungi that have microscopic algae living inside them. The algae make their own food by photosynthesis (like plants do), and they share it with the fungi. In return, the fungi provides the algae with a safe home.

Wet and wild

During the islands' warm season, the pampa isn't a sunny and pleasant place. It's raining hard most days, and every year around 8 ft (2.5 m) of rain falls. During the dry season, the misty drizzle coming in from the Humboldt Current makes the pampa even wetter than in the wet season.

8 ft (2.5 m)

Galápagos sedge

The pampa is home to some tough plants, and one of the toughest is the Galápagos sedge. Sedges look similar to grasses, but they have triangular rather than round stems and a different type of flower. They often live in wet places with poor soil where other plants can't survive.

Grounded bird

The pampa is a refuge for the Galápagos rail. A poor flier, this little bird lives on the ground, searching for insects and seeds in the undergrowth. Introduced predators such rats and cats have wiped it out in the islands' other habitats, and the wild pampa is now the only place where the rail can survive.

Galápagos tomatoes

The Galápagos Islands have many strange and exotic plants, including cacti that sprout from bare lava and giant daisy trees. Some native plants, however, are surprisingly familiar—meet the Galápagos tomatoes!

There are two species of tomato plants unique to the Galápagos. Scientists estimate that they evolved from a tomato species that arrived from the South American mainland less than half a million years ago. Unfortunately, after all this time, these two wild species are now under threat from a non-native tomato species brought to the islands by vegetable farmers.

Solanum galapagense

This Galápagos tomato species grows small orange fruits, which are around the size of cherries. The green sepals, around the top of the fruit, are always very long.

Long sepals

The tomatoes have tiny hairs.

Wild and tasty

The two Galápagos tomato species have been found on all the main islands. They are a favorite food of finches and tortoises, which spread the plant's seeds to new locations in their poop. There aren't many insect pollinators on the islands to help transfer pollen between the tomato flowers. However, the flowers of the Galápagos species are able to self-pollinate, which means they can make seeds—and new plants—without the help of pollinators.

Small and yellow

Wild tomatoes grow mostly in areas between the dry arid zones and Scalesia forests. They are found just about anywhere where there's plenty of sunshine and enough water. The plants are often seen on steep, rocky slopes high above the sea, where rainwater trickles down from higher ground.

Solanum cheesmaniae

This native species is called the Galápagos tomato. It produces small, yellow fruit around the size of grapes.

Short sepals

Smooth fruit

Other fruit

The warm conditions in the Galápagos are perfect for growing all kinds of tropical fruit. There are unique kinds of guava and wild passion fruit (above) growing here. Many introduced fruit plants, such as banana, avocado, and orange trees, grow here, too, in gardens and farms. However, most of the fruit and vegetables eaten by the islanders are brought by ship from Ecuador. Unfortunately, some of these species have entered the wild and are taking over from native plants.

Galápagos tomatoes are resistant to pests that attack tomatoes in other parts of the world.

Tomato plants grow on the rocky slopes of the shorelines of the Galápagos Islands.

Invader attacks

A wild cherry tomato from the mainland of South America, known as the "pimp," has escaped into the wilds of the Galápagos Islands. This species is not only taking over in some areas, but it's also cross-breeding with the native species, making hybrid tomato plants.

Protecting plants

The native wildlife of the Galápagos is under attack—especially the plants. The islands' natural plant communities are now overrun with species that have been brought in from abroad.

Some of these plants were introduced by farmers wanting to grow food. Others arrived by accident in imported cargo. Many have escaped into the wilds of the Galápagos National Park, where they are able to grow faster than native plants. The process is slower than with invasive animals, but introduced plants are changing the islands. They must be stopped! See the green panel on the next page to find out more about the native plants that are threatened.

Red quinine
This slow-growing tree was brought to the islands for making medicine. It's now spreading through the humid forests.

Rooting out the invaders

The best defense against unwanted plants is to dig them up, so they can't spread any farther. This is a difficult job that can take many years to accomplish. Conservationists on the islands are targeting the most damaging plants first.

Cuban cedar
Early settlers planted these big trees to use their wood for building ships and houses. Today, these cedar trees are taking over from wild Scalesia, especially on Santa Cruz.

Lantana
This big shrub produces pretty flowers. It was planted by gardeners in the islands' main towns, but it's now escaped into humid forests.

Hill raspberry
Originally from the Himalayas, this wild relative of the raspberry was introduced to the islands for its fruit and for its fast-growing thicket, used for fences. It now grows in thick bushes that crowd out native plants.

Elephant grass
Early farmers planted this tough, fast-growing grass as food for their herds of cattle. Today, it's outcompeting the native feather fingergrass.

Ancient tree fern

Ferns are an ancient kind of plant. They have been growing on Earth much longer than conifers and flowering plants. The world's first forests were full of giant ferns—known as tree ferns. There are still several hundred species of tree ferns left, but most are under threat from habitat loss and other problems caused by human activities. The Galápagos has its own tree fern, but it's being pushed out of its wet highland habitat by invasive quinine trees.

On the edge

One species of daisy tree, *Scalesia atractyloides*, was thought to have been wiped out by hungry goats. In 1995, however, five of these trees were found growing from the rocky wall of an old crater on Santiago Island. Even goats could not reach them here. The tree was back from the brink of extinction!

Native plants

Charles Darwin reported that many of the plants on the Galápagos Islands were "wretched-looking weeds." This is one thing he was wrong about. If you know where to look, the islands are home to some small but beautiful flowering plants, though many now need protecting. Native tree ferns need to be looked after as they are also under threat.

Galápagos rock purslane

These lovely pink flowers emerge from a spindly shrub. The plant is found only in the Galápagos and is at high risk of extinction in the wild.

Darwin's daisy

Although nicknamed a daisy, this small sunflower is found only on San Cristóbal Island. It has a close relative living on Española named after Robert FitzRoy, the captain of the HMS *Beagle*.

Common crinklemat

Low-growing with furry gray leaves, the common crinklemat covers flat, dry areas. After the rain, it produces a mass of tiny white flowers, which are an important food for lava lizards.

The islands were first recorded as the Galápagos on a world map from 1570.

People
and
preservation

The Galápagos Islands are a living natural history museum. People from all over the world visit the archipelago. They come to experience the wonders of nature and see for themselves the incredible ways in which life is always adapting and evolving to survive. However, the islands' wildlife has long been under attack from human activities. Today, visitors and residents of the islands are implementing new ways to restore the islands' damaged habitats and live in harmony with nature.

The shadows of tourists on Bartolomé Island, Galápagos.

Explorers

For most of their history, the Galápagos Islands were untouched by humans. Explorers finally reached here around five hundred years ago—and things began to change.

Damaging nature

Early visitors to the Galápagos caused a lot of damage to the wildlife. They drove some tortoise species to extinction (see the empty shells above), and the islands have never fully recovered.

People and preservation

The Galápagos Islands are not just a wild place filled with plants and animals. There are around thirty thousand people living on the islands as well.

The human residents of the islands, however, try their best to live alongside nature without damaging it. In fact, many of the islanders—known as Galapagueños—have jobs that help protect and preserve their islands' natural wonders. There's still a lot of work to be done. People have been living on the islands for around two hundred years now, and they have made many mistakes over the years. Today, the native plants and animals are under attack from invasive species that have been brought in from outside of the islands. The race is on to eradicate these invaders.

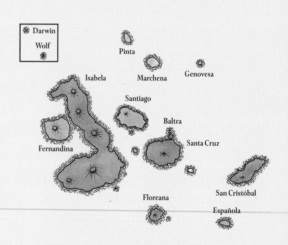

Inhabited islands

Only five of the islands in the Galápagos have people living on them—Isabela, Floreana, San Cristóbal, Santa Cruz, and Baltra. People visit the other islands, but they aren't allowed to stay there for very long.

Science

Thanks to Charles Darwin, the islands have long been a world center of scientific research. Scientists and researchers spend a lot of time studying nature in the Galápagos.

Conservation

The Galápagos need conserving, or looking after. There are many conservation programs in place to protect the land and ocean habitats.

Tourism

The biggest business in the Galápagos is tourism. People come to marvel at the famous animals and enjoy the beautiful scenery and tropical weather. Every visitor arrives by air from mainland Ecuador. The islands' tourism industry makes a lot of money for the country. However, so many tourists now visit the islands that they are in danger of destroying the natural wonders they have come to see.

Every year, visitors to the islands far exceed the amount of people living in the Galápagos.

Pirate paradise

The Galápagos Islands were discovered in 1535 when a Spanish ship sailing from Panama to Peru was pulled out far from the coast by strong ocean currents.

Aboard the ship was the Bishop of Panama, Fray Tomás de Berlanga. He and some of the crew came ashore to find water. They were the first people known to set foot on the Galápagos Islands. Berlanga was not at all impressed—he described the islands as a place where "God had rained stones." However, he did take note of the strange wildlife and reported that the birds were completely unafraid and had landed on his hands.

Pirate base

By the seventeenth century, the Galápagos had become a base for English and Dutch pirates. The pirates hid on the islands as they waited to ambush Spanish ships carrying gold and other treasures across the Pacific Ocean. The pirates captured giant tortoises for food, keeping them alive on their ships as a fresh supply of meat for long voyages.

Enchanted Isles

In 1546, Captain Diego Rivadeneira led an expedition to the islands. He called them the "Enchanted Isles" since they sometimes disappeared in mist and were hard to reach because the currents pushed his ships away. He wondered whether the islands floated on the sea and drifted from place to place.

Buccaneer Cove on Santiago is well named. It was once a popular refuge for pirates.

Incas

According to legend, the Inca emperor Túpac Yupanqui led a voyage of discovery to the Galápagos in the late fifteenth century—before European explorers had reached the Americas. The Incas ruled the western coast of South America up until Spanish invaders arrived in the sixteenth century. The Incas built boats by lashing bundles of reeds together.

Whalers

Oil made from whale fat, or blubber, was a valuable product in the nineteenth century. Whaling ships from all over the world sailed to the waters around the Galápagos Islands because they were a haven for many whale species. Whaler crews also came ashore from time to time to hunt the islands' fur seal, and almost wiped it out.

Settlers take over

The first person to live on the Galápagos was an Irish sailor called Patrick Watkins. He was left behind by his ship in 1807 and survived alone for two years. Soon, many more settlers came to live on the islands permanently.

By this time, the big business for sailors in the Pacific Ocean was hunting whales, or whaling. The islands were now an important place for making money, and countries fought each other to control the area. Whaling crews began to use the Galápagos as a place to rest and restock their supplies of food and water. For this reason, people began to spend more and more time on the islands.

Post office

In the early nineteenth century, a "post office" box was set up on Floreana. Homesick sailors visiting the islands left letters inside for other crews to take back for posting in Europe or North America. The original box has since been replaced and only tourists use it.

The real Moby-Dick

In 1818, American whalers found huge pods of sperm whales near the islands. The oil from these big whales was used in oil lamps. It didn't smell when burned and gave a brighter light than oil from other sources. It was the best oil of all the whales, but sperm whales were hard to catch. In 1820, the New England whaler *Essex* was sunk by a giant sperm whale near the islands. This inspired the 1851 book *Moby-Dick* about a battle between a sea captain and a fierce whale.

A better life?

In the 1920s, settlers from Norway arrived in the Galápagos, hoping to create a better life for themselves. They started a settlement in Puerto Ayora, Santa Cruz. However, not many of them stayed since they were disappointed by the lack of possibilities on the islands. In the 1930s, the population of the Galápagos began to grow. Some European settlers, mostly from Germany, came to the islands with the idea of creating a perfect society. They included a dentist who did not wear any clothes and only ate raw food! Unfortunately, he died from food poisoning. Another settler announced that she was the Empress of Floreana and wanted to build a hotel. She eventually disappeared and wasn't seen in the Galápagos again.

Ecuadorian islands

In 1832, Ecuador claimed the Galápagos Islands as part of its country. The first Ecuadorian settlements were on the islands of Floreana and San Cristóbal. They were prisons for rebel soldiers who had tried to take over Ecuador. The prisoners cleared forests and set up farms, but life was so awful that they frequently attacked the guards. The prisons were closed after twenty years.

Wall of Tears

Another prison was set up on Isabela in 1944. To keep the prisoners busy—and to stop them from plotting to escape—they were forced to build a stone wall. After fifteen years of work, the "Wall of Tears" was 300 ft (100 m) long, 20 ft (6 m) high, and 10 ft (3 m) wide. Many prisoners died during its construction.

Galapagueños

The people of the Galápagos are known as Galapagueños, and the towns and farms where they live make up just 3 percent of the total land area of the islands. The remaining 97 percent is the Galápagos National Park, which was set up in 1959 as a sanctuary for wildlife.

There is a military base on South Seymour Island—more commonly called Baltra Island—which was originally used by the US Air Force in World War II, but is now run by the Ecuadorian government. The capital of the islands is a small town called Puerto Baquerizo Moreno on San Cristóbal. The main industries in both towns are tourism and fishing.

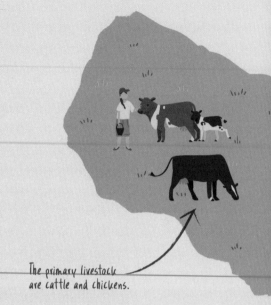

The primary livestock are cattle and chickens.

Horses were brought to the islands by settlers.

Farming

Farmland in the Galápagos is used efficiently. Care is taken to ensure that crops and livestock don't damage areas of wilderness. This map shows the types of farming carried out on Santa Cruz Island.

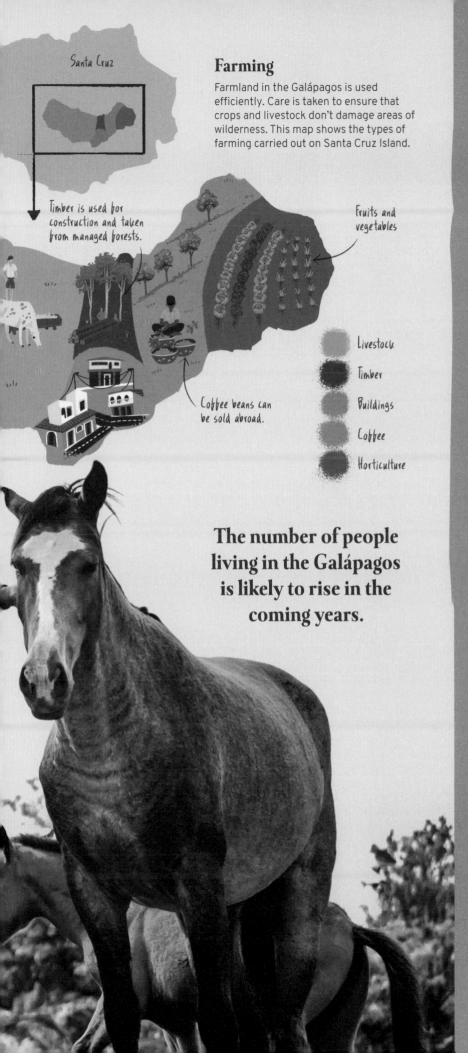

Santa Cruz

Timber is used for construction and taken from managed forests.

Fruits and vegetables

Coffee beans can be sold abroad.

Livestock

Timber

Buildings

Coffee

Horticulture

The number of people living in the Galápagos is likely to rise in the coming years.

Fishing

Many Galapagueños work in the fishing industry. However, the waters around the islands are a marine reserve, which means that the fishing boats must not catch too many fish. This ensures that there are enough fish for the penguins, sea lions, and other animals.

Food and farming

Farming is allowed on Santa Cruz, Isabela, San Cristóbal, and Floreana Islands. Not enough food is produced to feed all the islanders and visitors, so extra supplies are regularly shipped in from the Ecuadorian mainland.

Water supply

Tap water in Santa Cruz and Isabela is treated brackish water that's found at sites where rainwater travels underground from the highlands to meet the ocean. Floreana has a very limited natural water source from a natural spring in its highlands. Inhabitants of San Cristóbal use water from a lake in the island's highlands.

Waste problem

There are no landfill sites for the waste produced on the islands. Most of the waste is produced by the tourist industry. The waste tends to be burned, which releases poisons into the air and water. Some waste is dumped illegally, too, attracting rats and flies.

Goats

In 1813, the crew of a US warship left four goats on Santiago Island. They bred to become many thousands, outcompeting the tortoises for food. Eradication projects have now removed all the goats on Santiago and many other islands.

Fire ants

These ferocious ants from the South American mainland attack in groups. They kill small native reptiles and birds with their venomous stings and then eat the remains. The ants also attack tortoises by stinging their eyes.

Human damage

Unwanted fruit

Guava trees and other useful plants, such as blackberry and quinine trees, have escaped from farms and spread into the humid forests, taking the place of native plants.

The plants and animals that live on each of the Galápagos Islands have evolved to live together. When humans arrived on the islands, they upset this balance of nature.

Settlers brought animals and plants with them from other parts of the world. These non-native species escaped from captivity and began to live wild in the islands' habitats. Most of these species could thrive in their new home but only by destroying or outcompeting the native wildlife and steadily taking its place. Conservationists are now working to remove the invasive species and return the Galápagos to its former natural glory.

Cats

Arriving with the first settlers in 1832, cats hunt mostly at night. They kill many native birds and lizards. Conservationists are trying to eradicate the feral cats on the islands by using poisoned food.

Rodents

Invasive rats and mice arrived on the islands by escaping from ships. Rats are a particular problem since they eat the eggs and hatchlings of reptiles and birds. On Pinzón Island, no baby giant tortoise survived for fifty years, until black rats were finally removed in 2018.

Horses and donkeys

The nineteenth-century prison camp on Floreana used horses and donkeys as work animals. When the prison closed, the governor spread the animals to the other big islands.

Wild pigs

Pigs were first brought to the islands by the Ecuadorian settlers when they set up farms. The animals destroyed the ground nests of tortoises and birds. By 2006, wild pigs had been removed from several of the islands.

Growing towns

Towns in the Galápagos are getting more crowded and bigger as the population rises. The islands' quarries are growing larger to keep up with an increased demand for bricks for buildings. Local farms can't produce enough food for all the people on the islands, and every day thousands of crates of food and drinks arrive by air and sea.

Wild dogs

The descendants of pet dogs abandoned by early settlers have caused havoc by hunting iguanas and seabirds, including penguins.

Tree frog

The snouted tree frog—originally from the dry forests of Ecuador—arrived on the islands in 1998. Since then, it's spread through the lush shrubland areas, and no solution has been found to stop it.

Sea damage

Diesel fuel is brought to the islands in ships called tankers. There's always the danger of a tanker spilling its load and the fuel damaging the fragile sea life around the islands. The last time this happened was in 2019.

Protecting the islands

Keeping the wildlife and natural habitats of the Galápagos Islands safe from harm is a huge task.

Conservationists have been at work on the islands for almost sixty years. It's been slow progress, but the damage caused by early human settlers is gradually being repaired. Conservation teams have had to come up with some unusual plans to achieve this. They include the mass removal of invasive animals; use of biological control by introduced predators to prey on troublesome pests; and captive breeding of the islands' endangered species.

Charles Darwin Research Station

This is the headquarters of scientific research and conservation on the Galápagos Islands. The station is located on national park land that borders the town of Puerto Ayora on Santa Cruz Island. The research station has teams of conservationists working all over the islands and out at sea. They are there to figure out the best ways to protect the wildlife in the Galápagos National Park and Galápagos Marine Reserve.

Judas goats

Feral goats were a huge problem on the islands since they breed very fast, destroy forests, and eat all the native herbivores' food. To solve this issue, conservationists used "Judas goats" on Isabela and Santiago islands (between 1997–2006) to betray the location of herds of goats. (Judas was an infamous traitor from the Bible.) A goat was captured and fitted with a radio collar before being sent back into the wild. The conservationists tracked the Judas goat until it found a herd. Then, expert shooters arrived by helicopter and killed all the goats, except the Judas goat which was left to find another herd. Since 1997, more than 200,000 feral goats were killed on the islands by using Judas goats.

When caught and fitted with radio collars, Judas goats also had an operation to stop them from breeding.

Vampire flies lay their eggs in birds' nests. The eggs hatch into maggots.

Biological control

Insect pests are some of the hardest invasive species to fight. Conservationists are turning to biological control—in which another species is introduced to kill a pest. The maggots (larvae) of an invasive blood-sucking vampire fly are killing many bird chicks in the Galápagos. In 2018, researchers began to investigate a tiny wasp from mainland Ecuador, known only by its scientific name—*Conura annulifera*. The wasp is a specialist killer, only interested in this particular fly—and if it finds one, the fly won't survive!

Egg attack

When the maggot becomes a pupa—the inactive stage before adulthood—the tiny wasp strikes. It pierces the pupa's case with its spiked egg tube and lays an egg.

Adult wasp

Once fully grown, the wasp larva transforms into an adult wasp inside the fly pupa's case. It then breaks out and flies away in search of a mate and more vampire fly pupae to attack.

Living nursery

The wasp larva hatches and begins to eat the fly pupa. As the larva munches away, it grows steadily bigger.

Breeding back

The most endangered giant tortoises are being bred in captivity. This is the safest place for them until their home islands are free of invasive predators and competitors. Captive-bred tortoises were released on Española; the program was so successful that it was shut down in 2020 and the original breeding adults returned home.

90 percent of the reptile species in the Galápagos are unique to the islands.

Ecotourism

If the natural splendor of the Galápagos is to be saved for future generations, the islands need money—and a lot of it.

One way to get money is through tourism, and there are thousands of people willing to pay to visit these amazing islands. However, too many tourists will damage the islands' fragile habitats. One way to solve this problem is ecotourism. This type of tourism lets visitors enjoy the islands' natural wonders in a safe and responsible way, while the money they spend helps protect the islands and improves the lives of local people.

In 1978, the Galápagos Islands became a World Heritage Site.

Staying offshore

Many visitors do not stay overnight on the islands. Instead, they sleep on boats that are touring the islands and spend the days exploring new locations. Maybe a less expensive alternative is to stay in hotels on the islands and explore from there.

Guided hikes

Tourists aren't allowed to explore the Galápagos National Park—the protected areas of the islands—alone. They must join a tour led by an expert guide, who can explain everything the visitors need to know about the islands and their wildlife.

Water safari

The best way to see many of the islands' natural wonders is by boat. Tourists can swim with fish and sea lions, and see marine iguanas and seabirds in places that are hard to reach by land.

A valuable place

Everyone on the Galápagos Islands—residents and tourists—are taught why the islands are so amazing. Learning about this unique place makes people want to work harder to protect it.

Biosecurity

To prevent the spread of invasive species, there are strict rules on bringing food, plants, animals, and soil to the islands. Researchers are asked not to eat tomatoes, guavas, and passion fruit before visiting some islands in case seeds are left behind in their poop!

Glossary

adapt
how a living thing changes over time to help it survive better in its environment

adaptation
way in which an animal or a plant becomes better suited to its habitat

agriculture
growing crops and raising livestock for food

algae
plantlike life forms found in or near water. Seaweeds are types of algae

altitude
height of an object, living thing, or place above sea level

amphibian
type of animal that includes frogs and newts. Amphibians spend part of their lives in water and the rest on land

ancestor
animal or plant from which a more recent animal or plant is descended

aquatic
living in water

archipelago
group of islands

boundary
the point where one area ends and another begins

breed
when animals mate to produce offspring

camouflage
colors or patterns on an animal's skin, fur, or feathers that help it blend in with its environment

cetacean
type of marine mammal that includes whales and dolphins

characteristic
feature of a living thing or an inanimate object

climate
weather patterns for a particular area

cold-blooded
term that describes an animal with a body temperature that goes up and down to match the surrounding air or water temperature

colonize
take over

colony
large group of animals that live together

conservation
protecting environments and wildlife

conservationist
person that works in conservation

continent
one of seven large areas of land that the world is divided into: Africa, Antarctica, Asia, Europe, North America, Oceania, and South America

coral
soft-bodied marine animal that constructs a hard protective framework of calcium carbonate; they may form part of a larger coral reef

countercurrent
current flowing in the opposite direction to another current

crater
bowl-shaped depression, typically found near the top of a volcano

current
flow of water. There are many currents running through the oceans

DNA
short for deoxyribonucleic acid, DNA is a complex chemical that contains coded instructions, or genes, for living things to grow, develop, and maintain themselves. Different species have different genes

echolocation
system that uses sounds to find out about the surroundings, used by animals such as dolphins

El Niño

weather pattern that happens every few years in the Pacific Ocean. It makes the Galápagos Islands become drier

erosion

process in which rock or soil is worn away and removed by water and wind

evolution

process by which living things are able to change gradually over many generations, so they are better adapted to survive in a changing environment

Galapagueños

people who live in the Galápagos Archipelago

germinated

sprouted from a seed

gyre

a large system of rotating ocean currents

habitat

place where a community of plants and animals live

hotspot

place in the middle of a tectonic plate where columns of magma from the mantle rise up through the crust creating a volcano

insectivore

animal that eats insects

interbreed

when an animal or plant breeds with another animal or plant that is not closely related to it

invasive

term used to describe non-native species that are introduced into a new area and spread quickly. They are often hard to remove

lava

hot, molten rock that erupts from a volcano

larva

juvenile form of many animals, especially insects and amphibians

mangrove

large, tree-like plants that grow out from the shore into shallow seawater

marine

having to do with oceans and seas

mating

when two animals join together to create offspring

naturalist

person who studies wildlife and the natural world

organism

living thing

outcompeting

when one type of organism is taking over from another by eating all its food or using all its space

predator

animal that eats other animals as food

prey

animal that is eaten by a predator as food

pupa

resting stage in the life cycle of an insect, in which a larva develops into an adult

reptile

cold-blooded animal that has a body covered in hard, waterproof scales

scavenging

when an animal looks for and eats the remains of dead animals

specimen

animal or plant that has been collected as a record of its kind

tectonic plate

giant rocky plates that make up the Earth's crust

upwelling

ocean waters that rise up to the surface from depth; often rich in nutrients

Index

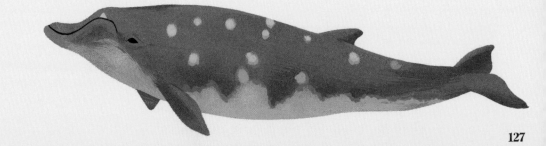

Author Tom Jackson
Foreword Steve Backshall
Illustrator Chervelle Fryer

Consultants
Animals Derek Harvey
People and preservation
Roslyn Cameron, Alex Antram
Plants Mike Grant
Geology Dorrik Stow

Acquisitions editor Fay Evans
Senior editor Carrie Love
US Senior editor Shannon Beatty
US Editor Mindy Fichter
Senior designer Elle Ward
Project art editors Charlotte Milner,
Charlotte Bull
Diagram illustrator Peter Bull
Editors Jolyon Goddard,
Abi Luscombe
Jacket designer Elle Ward
Special sales executive Issy Walsh
DTP designer Ashok Kumar
Picture researchers Laura Barwick,
Rituraj Singh
Production editor Abi Maxwell
Production controller Magdalena Bojko
Managing editor Penny Smith
Deputy art director Mabel Chan
Publishing director Sarah Larter

First American Edition, 2022
Published in the United States by DK Publishing
1745 Broadway, 20th Floor, New York NY 10019

Color illustration copyright
© 2022 Chervelle Fryer
Text and design copyright © 2022
Dorling Kindersley Limited
DK, a Division of Penguin Random House LLC
22 23 24 25 26 10 9 8 7 6 5 4 3 2 1
001–326014–October/2022

Printed and bound in China

For the curious
www.dk.com

MIX
Paper | Supporting
responsible forestry
FSC™ C018179

This book was made with Forest
Stewardship Council™ certified paper
– one small step in DK's commitment to a
sustainable future. For more information
go to www.dk.com/our-green-pledge

Picture Credits
The publisher would like to thank the following for their kind
permission to reproduce their photographs: (Key: a-above;
b-below/bottom; c-center; f-far; l-left; r-right; t-top)

Roving Tortoise Photos: Tui De Roy: 1, 4-5, 6-7, 14-15, 17 (tr),
19 (tr), 26 (cla) (bc), 27 (cb) (bc), 30-31, 32 (tl) (tr), 36 (bl), 36-7,
37 (br), 39 (bl), 43 (tr) (cr), (br), 50-51, 52 (br), 56-57, 58 (bl), 60
(b), 62-63, 63 (cra), 64 (cl), 64-65, 66-67, 70 (bl), 71 (tl), 76 (tl),
77 (tr), 80-81, 82-83, 89 (cra) (clb), 90-91, 93 (cra), 94-95,
98-99, 101 (tr), 104 (br), 105 (tc) (crb), 111 (tl), 116-117, 117
(cr), 118 (tl), 119 (cl) (bc) (br)

8 Dorling Kindersley: 123RF.com: Keith Levit / keithlevit (tr).
9 Alamy Stock Photo: Imagebroker (fcla); John Warburton-
Lee Photography (tc) ; Imagebroker (tl). Dorling
Kindersley: Dreamstime.com: Marktucan (tr); iStock:
Grafissimo (cra). Dreamstime.com: Danflcreativo (ca);
Martinmark (ftl). Shutterstock.com: NaturesMomentsuk
(cla). 11 Alamy Stock Photo: The Natural History Museum
(cr). 15 Alamy Stock Photo: Amar and Isabelle Guillen -
Guillen Photo LLC (cr); Nature Picture Library (tr). 16 Alamy
Stock Photo: Craig Lovell / Eagle Visions Photography (cr);
peace portal photo (tl); Doug Perrine (tr). Dreamstime.
com: Christopher Bellette (br). Shutterstock.com: Yvonne
Baur (bl). SuperStock: Antoni Agelet / Biosphoto (cl). 17
Alamy Stock Photo: Rosanne Tackaberry (clb). Dreamstime.
com: Steve Allen (cr); Jesse Kraft (bl). Getty Images /
iStock: Goddard_Photography (br); Paul Vowles (cla);
NNehring (bc). SuperStock: Gregory Guida / Biosphoto
(tl). 19 Getty Images / iStock: LuffyKun (tl). 21 Dorling
Kindersley: 123RF.com: Anan Kaewkhammul / anankkml (bc);
Dreamstime.com: Mgkuijpers (crb). 22-23 Alamy Stock
Photo: Daniele Falletta (t); Nature Picture Library (b). 23
123RF.com: juangaertner (tr). Alamy Stock Photo: Galápagos
(br). 25 123RF.com: tonaquatic19 (tr). Alamy Stock
Photo: Classic Image (cr); PhotoStock-Israel (tl). 27 Alamy
Stock Photo: Wolfgang Kaehler (cla). 28 Dreamstime.
com: Martinmark (tr). 32-33 Tropical Herping: Frank
Pichardo. 33 Dreamstimecom: Donyanedomam (tl). naturepl.
com: Paul D Stewart (tr). 34-35 naturepl.com: Tui De Roy /
Minden Pictures. 37 Alamy Stock Photo: Westend61 GmbH
(tl). 38 Dreamstime.com: Andrey Gudkov (tr). naturepl.
com: Maxime Aliaga (tl). 41 naturepl.com: Ben Hall (tl). 42-43
Tropical Herping: Alejandro Arteaga. 44-45 Alamy Stock
Photo: Imagebroker. 45 Shutterstock.com: Joel Bauchat
Grant (crb). 48 Alamy Stock Photo: Rolf Richardson. 49
Galápagos Conservancy: Diego Bermeo. 52 Dreamstime.
com: Roberto Dani (bl). 53 Alamy Stock Photo: Imagebroker
(bl); John Trevor Platt (ca); PhotoStock-Israel (br). 55 naturepl.
com: Ole Jorgen Liodden (tr). 57 Alamy Stock Photo: Minden
Pictures (tc). 58 Alamy Stock Photo: Steve Bloom Images (br);
WorldFoto (cra). Getty Images / iStock: mantaphoto (tl). 59
Alamy Stock Photo: AGAMI Photo Agency (tc); blickwinkel (tl);
John Holmes (tr); blickwinkel (ca). Getty Images: Sharif Uddin
/ 500px (c); Nadine Lucas / EyeEm (br). 61 Getty
Images: Sergio Amiti (c). 65 Alamy Stock Photo: Nature
Picture Library (crb). Getty Images: Keith Levit (cra). 67
naturepl.com: Pete Oxford / Minden (cb). 69 Alamy Stock
Photo: Sue Anderson (tl). 70 Alamy Stock Photo: David
Fleetham (tl). 71 naturepl.com: Pete Oxford / Minden (c). 72-
73 naturepl.com: Ralph Pace / Minden. 74-75 naturepl.
com: Alex Mustard (b). 74 Alamy Stock Photo: Reinhard
Dirscherl (tr); Science History Images (tl). 75 Alamy Stock
Photo: Minden Pictures (tl). naturepl.com: Shane Goss (tr). 76-
77 Alamy Stock Photo: James Stone. 79 Alamy Stock
Photo: Cultura Creative RF (bc). 80 Roger Hooper
Photography: (tl). naturepl.com: Alex Mustard (br). 82
Dreamstime.com: Gerald D. Tang (bl). 83 Alamy Stock
Photo: Don Mennig (bc). Getty Images: Stuart Westmorland
(tl). 85 naturepl.com: Brandon Cole (tr). 88 Dreamstime.
com: Burt Johnson (br). 89 naturepl.com: Brandon Cole
(c). Roving Tortoise Photos: Mark Jones (tl). 92 Alamy Stock
Photo: Hemis (tl). Dreamstime.com: Rui Baião (br); Angela
Perryman (bl). 93 Alamy Stock Photo: Wolfgang Kaehler (bl);
Roland Knauer (br). 95 Alamy Stock Photo: Danita Delimont
(cr). 97 Dreamstime.com: Andrey Gudkov (cla). 98 Alamy
Stock Photo: Andrew Linscott (ca). 100 Alamy Stock
Photo: Minden Pictures (tr). 105 Shutterstock.com: Andreas
Wolochow (tr). 106 123RF.com: wagnercampelo (cr). Alamy
Stock Photo: Ashley Cooper pics (bl); Zoonar GmbH (tr);
yomama (cl). 107 Alamy Stock Photo: BIOSPHOTO (bl);
MichaelGrantPlants (tl). 108-109 Alamy Stock Photo: Michael
S. Nolan. 110 Alamy Stock Photo: GRANGER (tr); Oldtime
(tl). 111 Alamy Stock Photo: Wolfgang Kaehler (b). Getty
Images / iStock: todamo (tr). 113 Getty Images: Michael
Melford (tl). 114 Dreamstime.com: Marktucan (cl). 117 Alamy
Stock Photo: Cannon Photography LLC (tr). Depositphotos
Inc: sunsinger (br). 118 Alamy Stock Photo: Minden Pictures
(tr); Krystyna Szulecka (cr); Minden Pictures (bl). Getty Images
/ iStock: samuel howell (cl). Shutterstock.com: Malcolm
Schuyl / Flpa / imageBROKER (br). 119 Alamy Stock
Photo: FLPA (cr). Dreamstime.com: Danflcreativo (tr). Getty
Images: MARTIN BERNETTI / Stringer (bl). Shutterstock.
com: RHIMAGE (tl). 120 Dreamstime.com: Donyanedomam
(tr). 121 naturepl.com: Tim Laman (bl). 122-123 Alamy Stock
Photo: robertharding

Cover images: Front: Roving Tortoise Photos: Tui De Roy

All other images © Dorling Kindersley

DK would like to thank:
Helen Peters for compiling the index
and Caroline Stamps for proofreading.
A special thanks goes out to all of our
contributors who helped make this book.

Author: Tom Jackson
is a leading natural history writer based
in the United Kingdom. As an author and
contributor he has worked on more
than sixty books.

Foreword: Steve Backshall, MBE
is a British naturalist, explorer, presenter,
and writer who has spent a lot of time
in the Galápagos.

Illustrator: Chervelle Fryer
is an illustrator hailing from the Welsh
capital of Cardiff. She finds inspiration in
flora, fauna, and traditional brush styles.

Photographer: Tui De Roy
is an award-winning wildlife photographer,
naturalist, and author of many books
on wildlife themes around the world.
She divides her time between the
Galápagos Islands and New Zealand.

Animal consultant: Derek Harvey
is a naturalist who studied zoology at
Liverpool University and has written books
on natural history and science.

Geology consultant: Dorrik Stow
is a geologist, oceanographer, and prolific
science author. He is Professor Emeritus
at Heriot-Watt University, and Distinguished
Professor at the China University of
Geosciences in Wuhan.

Plant consultant: Mike Grant
is a botanist and horticulturist who
works for the Royal Horticultural Society
as an editor.

**Anthropology consultant:
Roslyn Cameron**
is a long-term Galápagos resident who
worked as an educator for many years
before taking a more prominent role
in conservation.